T0406181

Financial Literacy and Money Script

Christine Sahadeo

Financial Literacy and Money Script

A Caribbean Perspective

Christine Sahadeo
St. Augustine Campus
University of the West Indies
St. Augustine, Trinidad and Tobago

ISBN 978-3-319-77074-1 ISBN 978-3-319-77075-8 (eBook)
https://doi.org/10.1007/978-3-319-77075-8

Library of Congress Control Number: 2018936515

Cover Credit: Micheal O Fiachra / EyeEm / Getty

Printed on acid-free paper

This Palgrave Macmillan imprint is published by the registered company Springer International Publishing AG part of Springer Nature.
The registered company address is: Gewerbestrasse 11, 6330 Cham, Switzerland

To my parents (deceased) Sookhranie and Dookin Ram
To my husband Ganesh Sahadeo

Acknowledgments

The decision to write this book has many beginnings or roots. Probably the most important was my mother's approach to financial independence (in particular with regard to her seven daughters), education, and managing one's life and happiness. My mother was determined that all her children had an opportunity of a good education. This was probably due to the fact that she was denied the opportunity to become a teacher, (owing to the Hindu tradition that females should not work) and wanted to ensure her children were successful, attained financial independence and seized the opportunities that she was denied. At home she taught us about savings, investing, putting aside for a rainy day, and understanding the word "bankruptcy" from an early age.

My learning and understanding of the importance of real estate also came from my mother. She proudly explained her decision to move from the lovely village of Surry, Lopinot, to Tacarigua, which had schools, religious establishments, easy access to public transportation, and most importantly allowed her children an education. I learnt from her that property is all about location, location, location!

In September 2006 as a Member of Cabinet I was privileged to be part of the decision to introduce a National Financial Literacy Program, which was introduced in the 2007 Budget of Trinidad and Tobago with the stated rationale, and I quote "The average consumer is now required to make complex financial decisions such as contracting mortgage and installment loans, choosing from a range of checking accounts and selecting savings instruments."

On leaving government, I joined the University of the West Indies in 2008 and I must thank the former Head of Management Studies, Errol Simms and former Principal, Professor Clement Sankat who approved the introduction of Financial Literacy to the University of the West Indies (UWI) and the partnership with the Central Bank of Trinidad and Tobago in 2010. I must thank the then Governor Ewart Williams for the support of this partnership with the Central Bank. I must thank Denyse Patrick who assisted in the early stages of this book and Tamara Rampersad, my research assistant, who provided tremendous assistance in proofreading the contents of this book. I must thank my son Avinash for his insightful feedback and critique.

The selection of topics to include in this book was a challenge. I have to confess that homeownership and entrepreneurship were included because of my own experience and saw them as fundamentally important in the life of every individual. Becoming an entrepreneur has always resonated with me. So when my young son at 17 wanted to start a business while still at secondary school, I supported the venture. The business has grown and albeit he is a chartered accountant and spent five years in the profession, he is now a full-time contractor and entrepreneur. My younger son is a born entrepreneur, and after leaving university he joined the family business and took it to new heights while starting his own business. Based on my own children's success, I wanted to assist others in becoming entrepreneurs. Accordingly the topics on entrepreneurship and preparation of business plans were included in this book.

In 1977 I suffered great pain on the loss of our home by fire which was not insured. My father had recently retired due to a medical condition and older siblings were encumbered with mortgages and family commitments. I was in a dilemma and had to change career options to one that would allow me to work and study. Being good with numbers, I gave up my first choice of medicine and began a career in accountancy. I frequently question if this was my destination or was it just karma? This however afforded me the opportunity to understand homeownership and debt financing. I had to secure a loan at the age of 19 and select, employ, and manage a contractor to build a two-story home. The construction of a two-story building although costlier than a single-story converted our home into an investment, the rental of the ground floor providing income to repay the mortgage. Homeownership is usually one of the biggest investments in one's lifetime and many times decisions are made without adequate knowledge or understanding of this investment. I saw this as an opportunity to include homeownership in this book as an important ingredient in acquiring financial knowledge.

The financial literacy program was very impactful at UWI and in 2012 it was also introduced as a co-curricular course. Although the topics included under this program are expansive, there are many subject areas worthy of consideration, such as preparation and understanding wills, personal income tax, and tax planning. We live in an ever-changing and turbulent world and it is becoming more imperative that we understand the basics in financial literacy so that we have the ability to make informed judgments and take effective decisions in the use and management of money.

Contents

1 A Review of Financial Literacy Initiatives in Selected Countries 1

2 Attitudes and Money Scripts, Goal Setting, and Budgeting 21

3 Saving and Investing 35

4 Debt Management 57

5 Planning for Retirement 67

6 Risk Management 81

7 Home Ownership 131

8 Introduction to Entrepreneurship 175

9 Basic Financial Accounting 207

10 Business Planning 231

Index 249

List of Figures

Fig. 4.1	Borrowing at the various stages of the family life cycle	59
Fig. 8.1	Main functional areas of a business	190
Fig. 9.1	The accounting process/cycle	214
Fig. 9.2	The T-accounts that would be affected	216

List of Tables

Table 2.1	Life cycle planning to achieve goals	29
Table 3.1	Share certificated environment versus non-certificated environment	42
Table 7.1	The stamp duty on residential land with house thereon	142
Table 7.2	The stamp duty on residential land only	143
Table 7.3	Stamp duty payable on mortgages: residential property (with a house thereon)	143
Table 7.4	Scale of attorneys' fees for common law conveyances and mortgages	144
Table 7.5	Scale of attorney's fees for transfers and mortgages under the Real Property Act	144
Table 7.6	Sample computation of attorneys' fees and stamp duty for the conveyance of residential property	144
Table 7.7	Attorneys' fees for the deed of release	144
Table 7.8	Sample computation of legal fees, stamp duty, and other fees for preparation of deeds of conveyance and mortgages (old law) for the following values	145
Table 7.9	Contracts to sign/execute	159
Table 8.1	Examples of links among the functional areas	200
Table 8.2	Procedure (including legal) for setting up a business in Trinidad and Tobago	201

1

A Review of Financial Literacy Initiatives in Selected Countries

Financial Literacy is the gateway to Financial Independence

The complexities faced because of the 2007–2008 financial meltdown made governments from all over the world undergo some introspection to determine what went wrong and how to prevent future pitfalls. After conducting research on their population, most governments believed that a main factor behind the financial crisis was the low level of financial literacy among their populace. The level of financial literacy is quite low in developed nations and even lower in developing countries. Thus, it was imperative for governments to implement policies and initiatives to increase the level of financial literacy of their citizens.

This chapter seeks to review the policies and initiatives of governments in the Caribbean including Trinidad and Tobago, Barbados, and Jamaica and internationally—New Zealand, Australia, the USA, and the UK—with respect to financial literacy and education. Financial literacy entails the ability to discern financial choices, discuss money and financial issues without (or despite) discomfort, plan ahead, and respond competently to life events that affect everyday financial decisions, including events in the

C. Sahadeo, *Financial Literacy and Money Script*,
https://doi.org/10.1007/978-3-319-77075-8_1

general economy (Orton 2007). A financially literate person must be able to make sound financial decisions regarding the use and management of money (Gale and Levine 2010).

According to Sonja Spiranec, Mihaela Banek Zorica, and Gordana Stokic Simoncic (2012), there are two distinct characteristics for financial literacy. They entail handling everyday financial matters and the ability to make the right choices/decisions based on available information. Adele Atkinson and Flore-Anne Messy's (2013) definition of financial literacy encompasses all the key concepts of financial literacy. In their research, financial literacy was defined as "a combination of awareness, knowledge, skills, attitude and behaviours necessary to make sound financial decisions and ultimately achieve individual financial wellbeing" (Atkinson and Messy 2013).

Financial literacy has become critical worldwide given the prevalence of personal overspending contributed in part by the improper and uncontrolled use of credit cards and poor corporate governance by companies due to the rippling effcts of such events, that it has been placed at the forefront for governments in both the developed and developing countries.

From mid-2007 into 2008 the world experienced a global financial crisis and a number of large financial institutions collapsed or were bought out, and there were several government bailouts. The reasons for the crisis have been well studied and analyzed and although the reasons for it are said to be numerous and complex, one major reason stands out: that is, the mispricing of financial risk. Investors and institutions took decisions on short-term gains (Gallery and Gallery 2010).

Trinidad and Tobago

In the 2007 annual budget presentation, the Former Prime Minister of Trinidad and Tobago the Honorable Patrick Manning highlighted the need for a comprehensive approach to financial literacy. Mr. Manning also the Minister of Finance and Head of the Cabinet said:

> Rapidly changing lifestyles have forced the bulk of the population to open bank accounts, to use ATMs, to own credit and debit cards and generally to participate actively in the formal financial system. The average consumer

is now required to make complex financial decisions such as contracting mortgage and installment loans, choosing from a range of checking accounts and selecting savings instruments. In too many cases, these decisions are made on the basis of insufficient knowledge and appreciation for the financial implications. This has been accompanied by a sharp increase in private consumption and rising consumer debt. Personal savings have in fact declined and with life expectancy increasing significantly many workers are ill-prepared for emergencies or retirement. This is not only so in Trinidad and Tobago but is in fact a worldwide problem. Accordingly, governments in both developed and developing countries are recognizing the need to promote financial literacy programmes to educate individuals to make better financial decisions. The Government is of the view that it is now critical that we launch a comprehensive National Financial Literacy programme to help our citizens deal with the basics of everyday financial management.

Launch of the National Financial Literacy Programme (NFLP)

On January 31, 2007, the Government of the Republic of Trinidad and Tobago (GORTT) officially launched a National Financial Literacy Programme (NFLP). The mandate was given to the Central Bank of Trinidad and Tobago (CBTT) to spearhead this very important initiative and work in tandem with the Ministries of Education, Community Development, Culture and Gender Affairs, and Legal Affairs, the financial sector, Non-Governmental Organizations (NGOs), and a host of organizations such as the trade unions and credit unions. The CBTT was identified as the most appropriate organization since the bank is capable of identifying gaps and other relevant issues that may arise in the market place. This action prevents any confusion that may arise between information and advertising since the CBTT has a high level of credibility in the provision of unbiased, impartial, and accurate information that is consistent with its supervisory and regulatory function within the financial services sector.

To ensure rigor and provide focus the CBTT established a new department to provide financial literacy training in Trinidad and Tobago. At the

"Commonwealth Committee on Financial Inclusion in the Caribbean" on August 28, 2012, the former Governor of the CBTT Ewart Williams said that although initially the financial regulator (CBTT) was a good choice, he opined that to expand and grow the program a separate entity is required with a singular mandate to deliver the program. Mr. Ewart Williams also confessed that he expected the program's reach to widen and be more impactful. The government launched the program to promote financial literacy, that is, educate individuals to make better financial decisions. According to Mr. Manning, the government was of the view that it is critical to launch a comprehensive NFLP to help citizens deal with the basics of everyday financial management.

The objectives of the NFLP are:

- To provide education on a range of issues related to personal financial management;
- To sensitize citizens about the importance of personal financial planning, budgeting, and informed money management so as to improve the quality of their lives;
- To provide the population, particularly the socially disadvantaged, with the tools and skills needed to handle basic financial transactions with confidence;
- To develop among citizens, a better understanding of the general financial environment, the products, services, and instruments therein; the opportunities they present for getting the most out of their finances and improving their financial well-being.

The Introduction of Financial Literacy Training at the University of the West Indies

The University of the West Indies (UWI), St. Augustine is the first tertiary education institution of its kind in Trinidad and Tobago to launch a financial literacy program for its students. This program (Financial Literacy: Train the Trainers Program) was introduced in the first semester of the 2010–2011 academic year. This financial literacy program was a joint effort between the educational institution (UWI) and the CBTT. The program was further enlarged to allow all participants to graduate as trainers of financial literacy and is referred to as, "Financial Literacy: Train the Trainers." This means that students are also trained in researching various financial products and making presentations and are expected to function as a vessel to transfer financial knowledge to family, friends, the elderly, schools, and communities at large.

The rationale for the introduction of this program at the UWI were many and varied. It is a misnomer that all university graduates are financially literate. Moreover only the students majoring in finance, accounting, and economics would really have some true exposure to financial issues, investments, and financial instruments. However, this financial literary training exposes participants to almost all the financial products and services internationally, gives a clear indication of how financial markets operate, and provides a clear understanding of the relationship between risks and returns. Therefore even students of accounting and finance at the university recognize the benefits and are participating in the program. In addition to this, students learn the importance of saving, investing, budgeting, goal setting, managing debt, homeownership, and planning for retirement.

By participating in this financial literacy program, the students are better prepared to make financial decisions, especially on leaving the university. Moreover in line with the UWI's mandate of "the Distinctive UWI Graduate," participants of the financial literacy course also add much credence to their degree. The UWI describes a "Distinctive UWI Graduate" as one who has a regional frame of reference and epitomizes the following attributes: a critical and creative thinker, a problem-solver, an effective communicator, knowledgeable and informed, competent, a leader, a team player, IT skilled and information literate, socially and culturally responsive, ethical, innovative and entrepreneurial, and a lifelong self-motivated learner.

This "Smart Money Financial Literacy Training" program was also introduced to support an existing program—Campus Chapter, Habitat for Humanity. The Campus Chapter works independently but also provides support for its sponsor, Habitat for Humanity. This partnership has provided the opportunity for not only social responsibility but also mentorship of our students. Habitat for Humanity builds homes for the underprivileged and also conducts training programs in areas of financial literacy such as budgeting, savings, and entrepreneurship. This training program is not only for the beneficiaries of the program but also for the communities in which they reside. Therefore in addition to providing labor, and building and financing homes, the program also allows the students to provide training in financial literacy to deserving communities. This means that students are equipped to serve the financial education needs of the community and are able to engage in service learning and meaningful community engagement.

The maximum enrollment figure for students pursuing the Train the Trainer course is usually 50. However, given the demand for the program, the first cohort comprised 67 students from the faculties of the UWI, St. Augustine and the second cohort comprised 68 students. Due to the rigorous structure of the program, only 60–70% of students graduated from the first and second cohorts. However, in order to maintain and add more credence to their certification, graduates are expected to conduct at least three to four training sessions each year at various groups in their communities. The CBTT also provides employment opportunities to graduates of the program.

The success of this program is so overwhelming that financial literacy is now offered as a cocurricular three-credit course each semester. Students pursuing this cocurricular course also graduate from the program and are given certificates upon completion. The financial literacy initiatives of the UWI are expected to be further expanded to include training for staff and the number of graduates from the initiatives is expected to drastically increase in the upcoming years. The importance of this program cannot be overemphasized given the low levels of financial literacy worldwide and given the recent global financial crisis.

The Collapse of Colonial Life Insurance Company Limited

The devastating effects of the recent financial meltdown which took place in 2007–2008 have also confirmed and justified the dire need to educate people on financial instruments and issues. After 15 years of consecutive positive economic growth, the Trinidad and Tobago economy declined in 2009 as a result of the global crisis and more specifically, the collapse of the Colonial Life Insurance Company (CLICO) Limited (Soverall 2012). Commercial giants such as CLICO Limited and its parent company, CL Financial Limited, suffered tremendous losses because of bad investment decisions and poor corporate governance structure.

Due to the sheer size and scope of CLICO's operations, the government's intervention was imminent to buffer the risk posed to the financial system. CLICO's operations contributed to 10% of the gross domestic product (GDP) in Trinidad and Tobago (Soverall 2012). Therefore, the government of Trinidad and Tobago had to engage in bailout plans to assist these companies and buffer the effects (loss of savings) of this heart rendering crisis. Individuals who invested in the various financial products and services offered by this commercial giant suffered losses.

A more financially literate public would have recognized the risks associated with the very high returns on CLICO investments when compared to the much lower returns offered by commercial banks. Any investor should therefore be wary in investing and more importantly in placing all one's investment in one financial institution. The financial literacy program in the areas of saving and investments carefully outlines the importance of understanding risks and diversification of one's portfolio. It was recognized that for these objectives to be met, the program had to target key groups such as students and young adults, employees in the workplace, community groups, and new and prospective homeowners. Primary and secondary school students were targeted given the widely accepted notion that financial education should be taught at a very early age so that the essentials of money management and good financial habits can be embedded early in their lives. Young adults were seen as a vital group since they are new to the work environment and are often faced with new financial obligations and the concerted advertising of financial products such as credit cards, loans, and insurance about which many are ill-equipped to make informed decisions.

Employees in the workplace, especially those over 40 who do not have ready access to financial and professional advice, were also targeted since it was noted that there is a need to encourage this group to focus on wealth accumulation and retirement planning. The CBTT saw the need to target community groups since this provides an avenue to reach a number of households and individuals who are at risk of financial exclusion. New and prospective homeowners, especially those obtaining homes from the government, were also seen as an important group since this category consists of low- to middle-income families who are now faced with a mortgage commitment that has to be included in their already limited monthly budget.

How Were Groups Targeted?

In its initial year of operations, students were targeted via financial education classes and employees in the workplace were facilitated through lunch-and-learn sessions approved by their employer. The NFLP sought to engage the wider population via the use of print and electronic media as well as through organized community sessions arranged by the community development officer of the area. In addition to these initiatives conducted in the initial year of operations, it is important to note that a financial literacy survey was also conducted during this time to obtain baseline information on the population.

Baseline Survey Conducted in 2007

During the genesis phase of the NFLP, the CBTT conducted a baseline survey in 2007 to evaluate the level of financial literacy of citizens in Trinidad and Tobago. Questionnaires were distributed and collected from approximately 1000 households by means of a randomized sampling technique which involved communities across Trinidad and Tobago. Respondents were asked questions pertaining to planning ahead, making ends meet, keeping track of their finances, and selecting financial products. Findings from the survey revealed vulnerable groups, showed that 36% of respondents were classified as having low levels of financial literacy. This survey also highlighted the need to concentrate the NFLP on areas such as budgeting, saving, investing, thrift, negotiating credit facilities, debt management, planning for retirement, planning ahead, financial fraud, knowledge of financial products, estate planning, negotiating mortgages, and starting and successfully operating one's own business.

Of all the aforementioned areas, "planning ahead" appeared to be the most crucial area that required particular attention. This was since the survey results illuminated the poignant reality that approximately 33% of persons over the age of 60 have pursued employment opportunities in order to obtain additional income to maintain an acceptable standard of living. Also, 54% of individuals who have retired did not have any occupational or personal pension plan. Furthermore 45% of the retirees reported that their current income was seen as inadequate and does not allow for a perceived acceptable standard of living in their retirement while 69% reported that the government pension (NIS/Old Age) would be their only source of income during their retirement.

Primary and Secondary Schools

The NFLP has targeted interventions both at the primary and at the secondary level of education. To date, the program has successfully reached every primary school (526) which comprises 476 public and 50 private schools. However, it is important to note that the interventions at the primary schools only targeted students at the standard two and three levels. At the end of the academic year 2007–2008, the program had reached 19, 500 students in 358 government schools in 608 classes. At the end of academic year 2008–2009, the number of students increased to 29,600 in 485 schools (447 government and 38 private) from 898 classes.

For the first term of the academic year 2009–2010, sessions were conducted at 120 schools (118 government and 2 private), reaching 9765 students through 279 classes. This primary school intervention is quite a successful and ongoing initiative. In the 2009–2010 academic year, the Ministry of Education agreed to and approved the incorporation of a secondary school intervention into the secondary school curriculum. The CBTT has worked in collaboration with the Ministry of Education in conducting several "Train the Trainer" sessions with secondary school teachers as part of this important initiative.

Public Interventions

The CBTT has implemented initiatives to reach members of the general public. The interventions take the form of face-to-face interaction, television, and radio advertisements as well as print media. Face-to-face interaction in the form of "Train the Trainers" program allows CBTT to reach diverse groups including employees, retirees, military personnel, security personnel, and religious and community groups. The CBTT is also working on an educational program for a television series. Other interventions include the use of short financial tips which are frequently published in printed media, displayed over a three-month period each time, on electronic public billboards. There are also a number of 30-second and 60-second ads that are aired on the radio and television. Pamphlets and booklets covering the content inherent in the financial literacy program are also published for public use.

Jamaica

Over the years, Jamaica and the Caribbean region by extension have been characterized as having societies with the lowest comparative saving rates worldwide. In Jamaica, there has been a significant increase in household debts coupled with the proliferation of credit card holders. There were over 300,000 credit card holders who formed about 10% of the Jamaican population in 2009. Like other parts of the region, these credit cards have been wrongfully used to fund normal day-to-day expenses. This obviously illuminates the heartrending fact that consumers are not properly educated on the responsible usage of this facility. Given these statistics, it is quite clear that consumers need to be educated on the use of credit cards to avoid falling prey to credit card debt misuse and abuse.

In addition to credit card misuse, the difficulties associated with saving in Jamaica are further perpetuated by increased hire purchase schemes and pay day loans. Hire purchase deals encourage the customer to purchase high-ticket items, repaying as much as three times the initial price of the item while pay day loans stifle the savings of consumers, trapping them in a vicious cycle of repaying high-interest loans from their salaries.

A quick glance at the Jamaican telephone directory will identify numerous enterprises offering consumers pay day loans that are borrowed against their salaries. This option to borrow is encouraged by these enterprises rather than borrowing from other financial entities such as banks and credit unions which offer a sound financial avenue that allows for the development of a more solid economic base.

The low level of financial literacy experienced in Jamaica can be attributed to the lack of thrift and saving among its citizens. Furthermore, there seems to be a lack of formal financial literacy programs which target primary and secondary school students as teachers focus only on an academic syllabus that has been provided by school administrators. This situation can be deemed an inadequate allocation of time and resources as numerous research has shown that the school environment provides an excellent mechanism to promote financial literacy. The earlier the financial literacy teachings are introduced in an individual's life, the more likely the positive saving behaviors can be developed and practiced.

Therefore, governments should seek to introduce financial literacy programs as early as possible in an attempt to aid in the development of positive money management behaviors which these students can later teach their own children. This method will ensure that good financial attitudes and behaviors are ingrained in the culture of the society. Financial literacy education is a lifelong learning. It is not an end in itself, but a step-by-step process. It ideally should begin in childhood and continue throughout a person's life until retirement. Early introduction of financial literacy programs during the childhood phase means that persons would develop the right attitudes to money and make more responsible decisions with regard to money.

Jamaica National Building Society (JNBS)

The Jamaica National Building Society (JNBS) is an organization that was established to promote greater saving and thriftiness among Jamaicans. This organization was formed in the post-slavery era with over 138 years of operation in Jamaica as well as the Caribbean regionally and internationally. In 1971, the organization supported the Government of

Jamaica by establishing a National Saving Committee and a public education program and training drive. The overarching objective of these initiatives was to encourage Jamaicans to become more a savings-oriented rather than spending-oriented community. According to the General Manager of JNBS, Mr. Earl Jarrett, the organization still functions as a social enterprise creating a significant impact in the lives of its target audience. With its focus primarily on saving and thriftiness, the organization has worked in collaboration with other firms and institutions to develop programs that seek to generate these ideals among consumers (Jarrett 2012).

At this juncture, one may question how a country with an organization that has over a century's worth of saving and thriftiness expertise and which was established with such a specific purpose can be struggling with debt and money management issues. Nevertheless, it is important to note that the JNBS has and continues to play an integral role in promoting financial literacy among Jamaicans. According to Mr. Earl Jarrett, the organization still functions as a social enterprise creating a significant impacting in the lives of people it comes in contact with.

The Caribbean Institute of Media and Communication (CARIMAC)

In 2008, the Caribbean Institute of Media and Communication (CARIMAC) highlighted the financial literacy concerns of the Commonwealth Secretariat to the JNBS. Given the organization's reputation and expertise, the JNBS appears to be one of the best organizations to approach in this regard. Hence, the JNBS was given an opportunity to collaborate with CARIMAC and the UWI, Mona Campus, to develop a financial literacy program. This two-year initiative had an impact on over 2000 high school students and was able to generate research data about students' attitudes toward saving. The final ceremony for the first year of the program accommodated approximately 500 high school students as well as their teachers. At the ceremony, students performed dramatic skits and songs to portray the financial knowledge they had acquired from the program. The program covered various topics including:

- Every Dollar Counts
- Balancing My Budget
- Running from Debt
- Expecting the Unexpected, and
- Business Planning

The JNBS also hosts regular community and members' meetings at various churches within these communities. The organization seeks to capitalize on opportunities to provide advice to persons attending any community-sponsored events. A saving product, "Affinity Account" was also developed to promote thrift in communities, churches, clubs, and other groups by returning an additional portion of the profit generated on the aforementioned account. For some time the JNBS has sponsored a weekly television program called "My Money and Me" on a youth cable station to provide useful tips on money management. The company recognizes that to keep young people intrigued in financial literacy programs, initiatives should be very exciting and attractive and tailored to suit the target audience.

With respect to primary and secondary schools, there is now a School Savers Programme that has 900 schools with approximately 120,805 students, whose accounts amounted to about J$369 million at the end of the July 2012 school year. Teachers play a very critical role in ensuring that this program is a success. They function as coordinators by collecting funds weekly, maintaining an onsite log of student savings, conducting financial literacy programs, and even operating as the medium through which funds are transferred to the JNBS. There is also a Baby Registry Account which encourages parents, with the support of relatives and friends, to start saving for their newborns as early as possible. With this account, parents are expected to continue plugging savings in the account until their child has reached the age when he or she can start saving on their own.

Barbados

The Central Bank of Barbados launched a National Financial Education Programme (NFEP) at the Frank Collymore Hall on Monday, August 31, 2009. According to its then Governor Dr. Marion Williams, the program seeks to educate Barbadians about how they can better manage their personal finances (Persaud and Persaud 2016). The governor explained that the bank would take a systematic and comprehensive approach to educating the average Barbadian, particularly about the basic best practices in managing his/her personal finances. To this end, the program will address an array of topics that are pertinent and relevant to personal financial management, including, budgeting and saving, borrowing and purchasing a home, credit and debit cards, insurance, retirement and estate planning.

The Central Bank of Barbados indicated it has intentions of working collaboratively with a number of organizations, institutions, and individuals who have already expressed an interest in the delivery of the program. The bank's main target will be the man in the street and will do so by hosting a series of "Lunch and Learn" sessions as well as by engaging in conversations with NGOs and community groups. The program will comprise presentations on budgeting and saving which will run for about three to six months before a new topic is rolled out. The campaign will also use the mass media to reach the public.

Although the initial phase of the program will target the adult population, the governor announced that the bank has hopes of collaborating with the Ministry of Education in the design of a program targeting school children. "The NFEP is not intended to create financial experts, but to get Barbadians to understand that effective management of personal finances would lead to an improvement in both their well-being and the country's," Governor Williams stated. "I hope that Barbadians embrace the programme and that we are able to change some behaviors" (Central Bank of Barbados 2009).

(A short review of financial literacy in New Zealand, Australia, and the UK is included to compare financial literacy programs at an international level.)

New Zealand

Research by ANZ (2009) and Widdowson and Hailwood (2007) revealed that New Zealanders generally have low levels of financial literacy, which has been reflected mainly in their inability to manage debt. In New Zealand, debt is a major problem since there are no limits to the amount of credit that individuals have at their disposal at any given period of time. Poor debt management coupled with economic recession and complex diversified financial products and regulations have spurred on interest by the government, institutions, and organizations to develop strategies to elevate citizens' levels of financial literacy. These aforementioned conditions have resulted in an overall increase in awareness and a greater appreciation for financial literacy in New Zealand.

At the inaugural Financial Literacy Symposium in Wellington in 2006, the development for a national strategy to raise New Zealanders' financial literacy was announced. However, their first National Strategy for Financial Literacy was officially launched in June 2008. This strategy outlined the procedures for improving, implementing, and evaluating the national strategy. To ensure rigor of the national strategy, an advisory committee was established to review the strategy and to monitor, implement, and also evaluate the national strategy. According to Taylor and Wagland (2011, 107), the three aims of the national strategy are:

- To promote flexibility and multiplicity of communications channels,
- To provide those most in need of financial education with appropriate programs, and
- To extend the delivery of financial education to as many New Zealanders as possible and sharing what works to improve the effectiveness of financial education.

There is now a growing concern regarding the retirement payment the New Zealand Government has to pay all its citizens. In New Zealand, there is a flat-rate universal pension scheme that is available to all persons 65 years and over irrespective of their employment status, asset, and income. The cushion provided by this scheme is capable of reducing the importance of private long-term savings, especially among lower-income groups and has the tendency to trigger a higher degree of investment risk-taking among higher-income groups (Crossan et al. 2011). Also, paid employment beyond age 65 is not penalized, which creates more opportunities for increased earnings and savings. The cushion provided by the universal pension and the ability to earn additional income beyond age 65 without incurring any penalty may suggest that financial literacy might only play a small role in the retirement planning of citizens. Nevertheless, there is a National Financial Literacy Strategy for New Zealand in which the Retirement Commission has been given the mandate to educate and inform citizens on retirement planning and financial management (Taylor and Wagland 2011, 106).

The onus is on the Ministry of Education to provide financial education in schools while other agencies provide financial education that is aligned with their areas of interest. New Zealand's Retirement Commission provides personal financial education to all New Zealanders via online, print, and mass media channels. These programs, however, target schools and the workplace using online mediums. At first glance, one can see that schools or workplaces that do not have access to Internet would be unable to access this valuable service. It is important to note that findings from recent research revealed that New Zealanders' financial literacy is not significantly associated with planning for retirement. As mentioned previously, a possible explanation for this is the existing cushion that is being provided by the universal pension system which creates a considerable level of retirement income security.

The most recent National Financial Literacy Survey conducted in New Zealand (Taylor and Wagland 2011, 112) revealed that there has been a substantial shift in the overall improvement in financial literacy when compared to previous results. Of critical consideration is the fact that given all the financial education programs, there appears to be little change in the knowledge level of vulnerable groups who are classified as having low skills, which suggests that more interventions are necessary to target these vulnerable groups.

Australia

Past research has indicated that in the next few decades Australia will experience a major shift in its age demographics resulting in an aged population. This can put an increased burden on the government since it may be forced to provide pension payments to a larger number of citizens in the future. To combat this inevitable problem, a compulsory Superannuation Guarantee Charge (SGC) was introduced in 1992 to address this high incidence of growing retirement. The SGC is an initiative whereby the employer has to pay a mandatory 9% from employees' salary toward their pension scheme. With the SGC, the onus is now on the majority of Australians to contribute toward their retirement. In order for Australians to understand the workings of the SGC, a financial literacy program which targets this initiative was introduced.

In addition to this, the Australian government established a Financial Literacy Foundation (FLF) in 2005 whose main purpose was to develop a website for Australians to understand money. This foundation was established since findings from the 2003 ANZ Bank Survey revealed that Australians had varying levels of financial literacy and young people had low levels of financial literacy. Therefore, this website for understanding money targeted schools and teachers and little emphasis was placed on adult financial literacy since this was left to the corporate and not-for-profit sectors (Guimaraes 2011). In 2008, the functions of the FLF were reassigned to the Australian Securities and Investments Commission (ASIC). According to Taylor and Wagland (2011, 114) this transfer was expected, "to strengthen ASIC's role in safeguarding Australia's economic reputation and wellbeing as well as to consolidate the government's commitment to increasing Australia's financial literacy." Another government initiative in 2008 was the establishment of a Financial Literacy Board which is responsible for providing advice to the government and the ASIC on financial literacy issues. There is also a Financial Literacy Resources Australia which provides a database of all the available financial education programs and resources that are available in the country.

United Kingdom (UK)

In the UK, the alternative term "financial capability" is used by the state and its agencies instead of "financial literacy" as used by many countries. The Financial Services Authority (FSA) in the UK started a national strategy on financial capability in 2003 and the UK also has a dedicated body to promote financial capability—the Money Advice Service. The Financial Services Act 2010 included a provision for the FSA to establish the Consumer Financial Education Body (CFEB). From April 26, 2010, CFEB continued the work of the FSA's Financial Capability Division independently of the FSA, and on April 4, 2011, was rebranded as the Money Advice Service.

The strategy previously involved the FSA spending about £10 million a year across a seven-point plan. The priority areas were:

- New parents
- Schools
- Young Adults
- Workplace
- Consumer communications
- Online tools
- Money advice

A baseline survey conducted 5300 interviews across the UK in 2005. The report identified four themes:

- Many people are failing to plan ahead.
- Many people are taking on financial risks without realizing it.
- Problems of debt are severe for a small proportion of the population, and many more people may be affected in an economic downturn.
- The under-40s are, on average, less financially capable than their elders.

The experts have expressed concern that unless steps are taken to improve levels of financial capability, UK citizens are storing up trouble for the future. However, it must be noted that there are numerous charities in the UK working to improve financial literacy, such as MyBank,

Credit Action, The Talking Economics Project, Citizens Advice Bureau, and the Personal Finance Education Group. Financial literacy within the UK Armed Forces is provided through the Money Force program, which is run by the Royal British Legion in association with the Ministry of Defence and the Money Advice Service.

Financial Literacy Training: A Global Perspective

Most governments have recognized the importance of financial literacy and have taken some proactive approaches to improve the level of financial literacy of its citizens. However many models have been adopted. Countries like New Zealand use the Internet to make financial product and services available and also use websites to transfer financial knowledge. This poses an inherent problem since persons who do not have access to Internet will be unable to access these services. Most countries have aging populations which result in large costs such as government pensions. The New Zealand government has a flat-rate universal pension scheme that is available to everyone eligible for pension irrespective of status, asset, and income. This provides a cushion as it facilitates a considerable level of retirement income security and citizens may not see planning for retirement as important as in other countries. In contrast to this, the Australian government has a compulsory Superannuation Guarantee Charge (SGC) pension scheme in which citizens contribute 9% to their pension plan and social security payments are determined by one's employment status, income, and asset. In many countries in the Caribbean, for example Trinidad and Tobago, a means test is used before a retiree can qualify for government pension.

References

ANZ. 2009. ANZ-Retirement Commission 2009 Financial Knowledge Survey – Summary (2009).

Atkinson, Adele, and Flore-Anne Messy. 2013. *Promoting Financial Inclusion through Financial Education.* Working Paper, OECD/IBFE Evidence, Policies,

Insurance, and Practice. https://www.wsbiesbg.org/SiteCollectionDocuments/OECD%20Promoting%20financial%20inclusion%20through%20financial%20education.pdf. Accessed 1 Sept 2015.

Central Bank of Barbados. 2009. Central Bank Announces Programme to Improve Financial Literacy Nationally. http://www.centralbank.org.bb/news/article/7515/central-bank-announces-programme-to-improve-financial-literacy-nationally. Accessed 2012.

Crossan, Diana, David Feslier, and Roger Hurnard. 2011. Financial Literacy and Retirement Planning in New Zealand. *Journal of Pension Economics and Finance* 10 (4): 619–635. https://doi.org/10.1017/S1474747211000515.

Gale, William G., and Ruth Levine. 2010. Financial Literacy: What Works? How Could It Be More Effective? http://ssrn.com/abstract=2316933. Accessed 1 Sept 2015.

Gallery, Gerry, and Natalie Gallery. 2010. Rethinking Financial Literacy in the Aftermath of the Global Financial Crisis. *Griffith Law Review* 19 (1): 30–50.

Guimaraes, Fernando. 2011. *Financial Literacy An Overview*. Pedia Press.

Jarrett, Earl. 2012. Address to the Commonwealth Consultation on Financial Inclusion and Literacy in the Caribbean Region, Port of Spain, Trinidad & Tobago. August 28–29.

Orton, Larry. 2007. *Financial Literacy: Lessons from International Experience*. Ottawa: Canadian Policy Research Networks Incorporated.

Persaud, Nadini, and Indeira Persaud. 2016. An Exploratory Study Examining Barbadian Students' Knowledge and Awareness of Costs of University of the West Indies Education. *International Journal of Higher Education* 5 (2): 1–20.

Soverall, Wayne. 2012. CLICO's Collapse: Poor Corporate Governance. *American International Journal of Contemporary Research* 2 (2): 166–178.

Spiranec, Sonja, Michaela Banek Zorica, and Gordana Stokic Simoncic. 2012. Libraries and Financial Literacy: Perspectives from Emerging Markets. *Journal of Business and Finance Librarianship* 17 (3): 262–278.

Taylor, Sharon, and Suzanne Wagland. 2011. Financial Literacy: A Review of Government Policy and Initiatives. *Australasian Accounting Business and Finance Journal* 5 (2): 101–125. http://ro.uow.edu.au/aabfj/vol5/iss2/7.

Widdowson, Doug, and Kim Hailwood. 2007. Financial Literacy and Its Role in Promoting a Sound Financial System. *Reserve Bank of New Zealand Bulletin* 70 (2): 37–57.

2

Attitudes and Money Scripts, Goal Setting, and Budgeting

Generally, individuals possess different outlooks when it comes to various aspects of their lives. Individuals have diverse beliefs and attitudes with respect to money, marriage, education, work, and friendship. This section will discuss attitudes and money scripts and the importance of goal setting and budgeting.

Attitudes and Money Scripts

An attitude is often described as a *settled way* of thinking or feeling about something. It is one's "attitude" toward a particular issue or circumstance that can influence one's behavior in any given instance. Therefore, attitude can be viewed as a main antecedent of derived behavior and resultant money script.

A Budget is used for planning and control—it is a commitment to an agreed outcome.

C. Sahadeo, *Financial Literacy and Money Script*,
https://doi.org/10.1007/978-3-319-77075-8_2

Attitude → Behavior

According to Hugh M. Culbertson (1968), most people seem to agree that an attitude involves at least three things, that is, an attitude object, the object being always something as defined by the attitude holder, a set of beliefs that the object is either good or bad, and a tendency to behave toward the object so as to keep or get rid of it. An "attitude object" is simply the item being thought of, for instance education or money, and it is defined by the attitude holder. The individual has a set of beliefs that the "attitude object" is either good or bad. A person has a tendency to behave a certain way toward the "attitude object" given his/her particular set of beliefs about the object.

Money has often been used as a source of tension for individuals (Goldberg and Lewis 1978). Some of the main motives for acquiring and using money are for security, power, love, and freedom (Goldberg and Lewis 1978). Thomas Li-Ping Tang (1992) summarized six beliefs representing the areas of affective, cognitive, and behavioral attitudes toward money. Tang (1992) stated that money was believed to be (1) good, (2) evil, (3) represent achievement, (4) a sign of respect, (5) a sense of power, and (6) important to budget. Kent T. Yamauchi and Donald J. Templer (1982) say that individuals may have the attitude and belief that money is a symbol of success or status. However, it is in those attitudes and beliefs that the whole notion of money scripts begins.

"Money scripts" is a term coined by financial psychologists Brad Klontz and Ted Klontz (2009), to describe an individual's core beliefs about money that drive their behavior. According to these researchers, money scripts are beliefs that are typically unconscious, developed during childhood, passed down from generation to generation within families and cultures, contextually bound, and often only contain partial truths (Klontz and Klontz 2009).

Money scripts are at the core of all our financial behaviors, both beneficial and problematic. According to Bradley Klontz and Sonya Britt (2012), the pattern of one's money script can predict disordered money behaviors, such as financial infidelity, compulsive buying, pathological gambling, compulsive hoarding, financial dependence, and financial enabling. Klontz and Britt (2012) also viewed an individual's profession as a determinant of his/her money script patterns and vulnerability to disordered money behaviors. For instance, in comparison to financial advisers, mental health professionals are more likely to be money avoidant, business professionals tend to be anxious and secretive around money, and business professionals, mental health professionals, and educators are more likely to avoid thinking about money, try to forget about their financial situation, and avoid looking at their bank statements (Klontz and Britt 2012).

Money scripts that are developed in response to an emotional flashpoint characterized by significant losses such as the Great Depression, parental abandonment, or financial bailouts by a family member can become resistant to change even when they are self-destructive (Klontz and Klontz 2009). Nevertheless, once money scripts are identified, they can be challenged and changed to interrupt destructive financial patterns and promote financial health (Klontz and Britt 2012).

Researchers have identified four main categories of money scripts, namely, money status, money worship, money avoidance, and money vigilance (Klontz et al. 2011). Three of these are linked to poor financial health (Klontz et al. 2011) and are associated with lower levels of net worth, lower income, and higher amounts of revolving credit (Klontz and Britt 2012).

However, this chapter seeks to divide these money scripts as well as other scripts into two broad headings:

(a) Healthy money scripts
(b) Unhealthy money scripts

Healthy Money Scripts

These scripts are often referred to as healthy since they result in financial behaviors that can positively affect our lives. Some examples of healthy money scripts are:

(i) Be grateful for what you already have.
(ii) Honesty is the best policy.
(iii) Enhance yourself and others.
(iv) Maintain a positive outlook on life.

These Healthy Money Scripts are described as follows:

(i) **Be grateful for what you already have**
Individuals with this type of money script are usually satisfied with their financial status and do not see the need to engage in financial greed.

(ii) **Honesty is the best policy**
With this money script, individuals believe honesty is the key to financial success. They conduct all financial endeavors ethically and view the engagement in financial schemes negatively.

(iii) **Enhance yourself and others**
Individuals with this type of money script often engage in philanthropic behaviors. They tend to engage in volunteerism and view the enhancement of others just as important as the enhancement of oneself. They are usually selfless and their main focus is not on their personal financial gain.

(iv) **Maintain a positive outlook on life**
This money script encourages you to remain balanced and work positively with challenges. Having goals and objectives can help an individual maintain a positive outlook.

Unhealthy Money Scripts

Scripts are often referred to as unhealthy if they result in financial behaviors that can negatively affect our lives. Some examples of unhealthy money scripts are:

(i) Money status,
(ii) Money worship, and
(iii) Money avoidance.

These Unhealthy Money Scripts are described as follows:

(i) **Money status**
With this script, the underlying beliefs are net worth and self-worth which are synonymous, and people are only as successful as the amount of money they earn (Klontz and Britt 2012). Individuals

who possess this money script pretend to have more money than they actually do, which results in a greater risk of overspending in an effort to give people the impression that they are financially successful (Klontz and Britt 2012). According to Klontz and Britt (2012), they also believe that if they live a virtuous life, the universe will take care of their financial needs.

Individuals with this type of money script display compulsive spending behaviors and are pathological gamblers who gamble in an attempt to win large sums of money to prove their worth to themselves and others (Klontz and Britt 2012). They are also dependent on others financially, lie to their spouse about spending, and usually have lower net worth and income (Klontz and Britt 2012). This money script is unhealthy since it results in individuals accumulating unnecessary debt and paralyzes their ability to save.

(ii) **Money worship**

Individuals who possess this money script believe that money is the key to happiness and more money will solve all problems (Klontz and Britt 2012). They believe that one cannot have enough money and will never really be able to afford all the things they want in life (Klontz and Britt 2012). According to Klontz and Britt (2012), the tension between believing that more money and things will make one happier and the sense that one will never have enough money can result in chronic overspending in an attempt to buy happiness.

Individuals who possess this type of money script are more likely to have lower income and net worth and are often trapped in a cycle of revolving credit card debt (Klontz and Britt 2012). They spend compulsively, hoard possessions, place work ahead of family, try to ignore their financial situation, give money to others even when they cannot afford it, and are financially dependent on others (Klontz and Britt 2012).

(iii) **Money Avoidance**

With this script, the underlying belief is that money is a source of fear, anxiety, or disgust (Klontz and Britt 2012). Individuals with this type of script believe money is bad; rich people are greedy, corrupt, they do not deserve money, and there is virtue in living with less money (Klontz and Britt 2012). Money avoiders also hold conflicting beliefs that having more money could end their problems and improve their self-worth and social status (Klontz and Britt 2012). Therefore, they may vacillate between the extremes of holding great contempt for money and people of wealth and placing too much value on the role of money in their own life satisfaction (Klontz and Britt 2012). According to Klontz and Britt (2012), money avoiders may sabotage their financial success or give money away in an unconscious effort to have as little as possible, while at the same time they may be working excessive hours in an effort to make money. This type of money script is associated with poor financial health and individuals with this script tend to have less money and lower net worth (Klontz and Britt 2012).

Money avoiders are guilty of hoarding, overspending and compulsive spending, depending financially on others, sacrificing their financial well-being for the sake of others, avoiding to look at their bank statement, unable to stick to a budget, and trying to forget about their financial situation (Klontz and Britt 2012).

Examples of unhealthy money scripts include:

- There will never be enough money.
- More money will make us happy.
- Money will give me meaning.
- Money is the root of all evil.
- Money was made to be spent; tomorrow will take care of itself.
- I must get rich by any means.
- I do not believe in owning money.
- It is not nice or necessary to talk about money.
- Making a will is inviting death.
- I do not trust anyone around money.
- I am good and the Universe will take care of me.
- Money is not important.

Money Vigilance: Elements of Both Healthy and Unhealthy Features

There also exists the possibility for a money script to have both positive and negative aspects. This is evident with persons whose script is money vigilant. Individuals who possess this money script believe saving is important and people should work for their money and not be given handouts (Klontz and Britt 2012). According to Klontz and Britt (2012), they are alert, watchful, and concerned about their financial welfare. They usually pay for items in cash, are less likely to buy on credit, and have higher income and net worth (Klontz and Britt 2012).

Individuals with this type of script tend to be overly anxious and secretive about their financial status with individuals who are not closest to them, are significantly less likely to spend compulsively, gamble excessively, enable others financially, and ignore their finances (Klontz and Britt 2012). Although some aspects of this script are healthy in terms of emphasis being placed on savings and frugality, it is sometimes viewed as unhealthy when excessive wariness or anxiety inhibits one's ability to capitalize on investment opportunities and enjoy the benefits and sense of security that money can provide (Klontz and Britt 2012).

Goal Setting: The Importance of Goal Setting

A goal is a statement about some expected future state or outcome. Goal setting is clearly defining exactly what you want and understanding why you want it. It is very important in order to achieve one's aspirations. They help focus your efforts on the things you really want in life. By following the five golden rules of goal setting you can set goals with confidence and enjoy the satisfaction that follows when you accomplish your goals.

The five golden rules of goal setting are:

1. Set goals that motivate you.
2. Set SMART goals.
3. Set goals in writing.
4. Make an action plan.
5. Stick with it.

Setting S.M.A.R.T. Goals

Emphasis must be placed on the importance of setting goals that are, **S**pecific, **M**easurable, **A**ttainable, **R**elevant, and **T**ime-bound (S.M.A.R.T). According to H.A. Schut and H.J. Stam (1994), the acronym can be broken down as follows:

- **Specific**—it must be clear and well defined and able to be broken into smaller steps.
- **Measurable**—it refers to including precise amounts and dates so that success can be assessed.
- **Attainable**—it has to do with the possibility of achieving the goal one has set.
- **Realistic/Relevant**—it should be in line with your life and career.
- **Time-bound**—it concerns setting deadlines.

Therefore, an example of a S.M.A.R.T goal is "I would like to complete my B.Sc. Accounting degree as a full-time student in the next three (3) years."

Setting Goals Using Different Time Frames

There are short-term goals, medium-term goals, and long-term goals. It is important that individuals differentiate among these goals since each may require different strategies and effort to ensure they are accomplished.

Short-term goals are those you plan to achieve in one to two years (e.g., immediately owning a life insurance policy worth $400,000). Medium-term goals are those you plan to achieve in three to five years (e.g., saving $30,000 in five years to pay down on a house costing $300,000), and long-term goals are those you would like to achieve beyond a five-year period. An example of a long-term goal is planning to retire at 60 years with retirement income of $15,000 each month.

Generally when setting goals, individuals will need to focus on goals that matter, narrow their objectives, be prepared for conflicting goals, put time on their side by making age a factor, choose carefully, and include family members. Age is a very important component when selecting goals: from 18 to 35 years is known as the accumulation stage of an individual's life, 35–40 years is referred to as consolidation, and 56–60 years relates to preservation. Please refer to Table 2.1.

Goal Setting Versus Dreaming

Individuals must be able to differentiate between goal setting and dreaming. The difference between a goal and dream is essentially a deadline. Goals are usually very attainable once they are planned and proper execution strategies are employed. They are the desired results a person envisions, plans, and commits to achieve. Goals are usually focused and specific. However, dreaming entails hoping for an accomplishment that is far-fetched and highly unlikely to be attained. It is fantasizing on what we would love but realistically may never have. Dreams are unfocused and non-specific. An example of a dream is a low-income earner wishing for a mansion.

Table 2.1 Life cycle planning to achieve goals

Life cycle	Needs	Time frame
18–35 years (Accumulation)	Education Home/vehicle Start retirement planning Emergency fund	Short term
35–50 years (Consolidation)	Children's college Vacation Planning for retirement	Medium term
50–60 years (Preservation)	Preparing for retirement Lifestyle changes	Long term
>60 years	Estate planning Gifting	Distant (>15–20 years)

Compulsory Goals Versus Optional Goals

Compulsory goals are those that should take precedence in the lives of individuals. The education of oneself and children, planning for retirement, and family planning can be considered compulsory goals. In contrast to this, optional goals are those that are not a priority such as a luxury car, vacation abroad, upgrading of residence, purchasing luxury items for home, and charity (religious or social). Individuals must be very prudent and be able to distinguish between compulsory and optional goals since they both have differing impacts on the lives of individuals. It is recommended that compulsory goals should take precedence over optional goals since these have a more long-lasting effect in the lives of individuals.

Budgeting

A budget is a money plan that helps you organize and control your financial resources and set and realize financial goals. It is the planned allocation of available funds which can be used as a guideline for saving and spending. Budgeting involves outlining all sources of income, capital payments, and expenses. It provides an opportunity to seek ways to earn additional income. It can be used as a barometer to manage and curtail expenses. To ensure a budget is realistic and attainable one must budget for fixed expenditures such as loan repayment, rent, and insurance before budgeting for other expenses. A budget should be based on needs and not wants. A budget should pay oneself first, that is, treat personal savings as an expense. A budget should have limited flexibility to ensure commitment to agreed outcomes. It is also important to differentiate between needs and wants. A need is something you cannot do without, for example, food, clothing, and shelter. In contrast to this, a want is something you would like to have; it is not absolutely necessary—it may be a good thing to have but not necessary, for example, a music set, an expensive phone, or laptop.

Generally, there are three main steps in creating an actual budget:

1. Calculate all available sources of income. For example, permanent job salary, income from hobbies and other activities such as tutoring, hair-dressing, tailoring, promotions, and bartending.
2. Detail expenses by type. For instance, expenses can be categorized as fixed and variable. Fixed payments and expenses are costs that are compulsory, such as loan installments, insurance premiums, rent, insurance, cable bill, and water. However, it is important to note that although some expenses are considered fixed, they are subject to change over time but remain constant for a relatively long period. In contrast to this, variable expenses include entertainment, travel, and food.
3. Determine the type of budget you have prepared and take the necessary actions. There are three main types of budget—surplus, deficit, and balanced budget. A surplus budget exists when income exceeds expenditure. Individuals with this type of budget can use excess income to save for future endeavors, to pay off pending debt, or make purchases that have been delayed.

   In contrast to this, a deficit budget is a situation where expenditure exceeds revenue. Individuals with a deficit budget may have to find ways to decrease their expenses and increase income. For example, using telephone sparingly, seeking cheaper interest rates on loans, bulk buying with friends and relatives, avoiding junk food, reusing and recycling, carpooling to work, and asking for discounts. Expense reduction strategies can be used to ensure a surplus or balanced budget. Where loan repayments are high and unmanageable, restructuring of debt or consolidation of debt can reduce the deficit but requires discipline to prevent a resurgence of excess debt. With increasing expenditure daily, individuals must acquire skills and training in order to obtain new sources of income. Some of the strategies may include acquiring additional skills, using available skills to earn additional income, earning extra money from hobbies, encouraging spouse to gain extra employment, and seeking safe investment opportunities.

A budget is considered balanced when income and expenses are equal. In other words, there is no surplus or deficit. However the main reason for budgeting is to plan and control and ensure a level of savings for future needs. It is important to note that some budgets (government) are considered cyclically balanced budgets when they are not necessarily balanced from year to year but are balanced over the economic cycle.

A major benefit of budgeting is the control element—comparing actual expenditure with budget and taking corrective action as necessary. Variances between budget and actual forces one to reflect and either relook the budgeting process or curb spending if necessary. This is the real benefit of budgeting—planning and making responsible decisions regarding saving, investing, and spending. There are numerous benefits that can be derived from budgeting. A budget helps you control and keep track of spending, shows precisely how money is spent, and helps to identify money for saving and investment. It is a planning tool that reveals inefficient and/or inappropriate spending habits and inadequate savings and should redirect and motivate you to reset goals.

When budgeting, it is also important that individuals be mindful of capital and recurrent expenditure. Capital expenditure refers to costs incurred to create some future economic benefit such as purchase of home, capital improvements to home, or purchase of car. In contrast to this, recurrent expenditure refers to costs which do not result in the creation, acquisition, or upgrade of fixed assets.

References

Culbertson, Hugh M. 1968. What Is an Attitude? *Journal of Cooperative Extension* VI (2): 79–84.

Goldberg, H., and R.T. Lewis. 1978. *Money Madness: The Psychology of Saving, Spending, Loving and Hating Money*. New York: William Morrow and Company, Inc.

Klontz, Bradley, and Sonya Britt. 2012. How Clients' Money Scripts Predict Their Financial Behaviors. *Journal of Financial Planning* 25: 33–43.

Klontz, Brad, and Ted Klontz. 2009. *Mind over Money: Overcoming the Money Disorders that Threaten Our Financial Health*. New York: Broadway Business.

Klontz, Bradley, Sonya L. Britt, Jennifer Mentzer, and Ted Klontz. 2011. Money Beliefs and Financial Behaviors: Development of the Klontz Money Script Inventory. *Journal of Financial Therapy* 2 (1): 1–22.

Schut, H.A., and H.J. Stam. 1994. Goals in Rehabilitation Teamwork. *Disability Rehabilitation* 16: 223–226.
Tang, Thomas Li-Ping. 1992. The Meaning of Money Revisited. *Journal of Organizational Behavior* 13 (2): 197–202.
Yamauchi, Kent T., and Donald J. Templer. 1982. The Development of a Money Attitude Scale. *Journal of Personality Assessment* 46 (5): 522–528.

3

Saving and Investing

The Importance of Saving: *Savings Is a Habit, Savings is a Commitment*

Some mathematicians may say that the following equations are the same owing to the commutative property of equations, that is:

1. ***Income – Savings = Expenses***
2. ***Income – Expenses = Savings***

However the consequences arising from these two equations can be very different. The rationale for the first equation is that savings should be a decision based on a goal and savings is put aside first and the residual used to pay expenses. In the second equation savings is the residual, if any, after paying expenses. Savings is income not spent or deferred consumption. It involves putting aside money from current income on a regular basis for a specific purpose or goal. Some methods of saving include old-fashioned systems such as using a piggy bank and participating in a

Be financially independent, build wealth—master the art of saving and investing, and watch your money work for you.

C. Sahadeo, *Financial Literacy and Money Script*,
https://doi.org/10.1007/978-3-319-77075-8_3

sou-sou, saving through a financial institution via joint accounts, a range of savings accounts, and saving by investing in a pension plan. Financial institutions include banks, trust companies, credit unions, and other investment companies. The selection of a financial institution for investment depends on a number of factors including rate of return, charges, location, level of customer service, and types of accounts on offer.

Commercial banks offer a range of accounts to save money including Ordinary Savings Account, Current Account, Time Savings Deposit Account, and Foreign Exchange Deposits. Ordinary Savings Accounts allow you to access your money at any time and the interest rate it carries is generally low. Interest is paid on the average balance kept in the account for the month. Current Accounts allow you to write checks which is useful in particular if you are operating a business. Normally it does not pay interest although some may pay interest if the account balance is greater than a pre-specified amount. This type of account may carry a service charge.

A Time Savings Deposit Account is similar to a Fixed Deposit. The money must be left for a period of time whereby interest rates are progressively higher for larger deposits and those placed for longer periods. When the account is opened, the time, amount, and interest rate will be agreed with the bank and constitutes a contract which has implications if the deposit is cashed in at an earlier date. If you request repayment of deposit before the pre-appointed time, most of the interest earned would not be paid for breach of contract.

Most financial institutions offer deposits account in currencies other than the country's currency. Savings in credit unions operate via membership arrangements. Deposits of funds are deemed to be shares purchased and not termed "deposits" as in banks and other financial institutions. A member of the credit union does not receive interest income but rather a dividend, a share of the profit of the institution. Credit unions generally offer lower interest rates than commercial banks as shares are used as collateral for the loan and therefore loans are also more accessible to the members.

Savings for one's retirement is necessary if we want to maintain our standard of living. Pensions from employment are generally inadequate to support the same standard of living prior retirement. An employer's pension plan is a type of retirement plan whereby the employer and employee both make contributions to the plan. This pool of retirement funds is then invested on the employee's behalf, allowing them to receive benefits upon retirement.

There are basically two types of employers' pension plan. These are a defined benefit pension plan and a defined contribution plan. Employees need to know the difference between both plans in order to sufficiently plan for retirement. With a defined benefit plan, the employer guarantees that the employee will receive a definite amount of funds upon retirement, regardless of the performance of the investment pool. On the other hand, with a defined contribution plan, the employer makes predefined contributions along with the employee's contribution, but the final amount of benefit received by the employee depends on the performance of the invested pool.

Job stability has become a more pressing issue in recent times. In many situations employers offer contract employment with payments of gratuity instead of pension and the individual ideally should use these funds for investment in a retirement fund. An employee may not be able or willing to keep the said job for a number of years and this has repercussions for pension arrangements. Given the nature of today's employment, individuals who are self-employed or employed but unable to join an employers' pension plan (contract and temporary workers), can start a personal pension plan to cater to their retirement needs. Unlike an employer's pension plan, a private pension plan is managed by an insurance company or an investment firm which invests this retirement pool to provide future benefits for investors. A private pension plan can also be enjoyed by individuals who already have an employer's pension plan but still see the need to further invest in a private plan to ensure their standard of living is sustained. There are also many tax benefits for individuals for investing in annuities and pension plans as government's social cost will be substantially less if citizens do not depend on the government's budget for their pension.

Saving is important to purchase capital items such as a house, property, land, and car. Capital items are acquired in order to leave a legacy to children and grandchildren; to educate self and/or children; to earn interest from investments such as starting a business; to plan for retirement; and to secure emergency funds in case of eventualities. Numerous factors determine our level of saving, such as our awareness of future uncertainties (e.g., illness and job retrenchment), level of wages, habits (e.g., if frugal, savings will be high), level of reckless spending, preparation for retirement, and government policies (e.g., National Insurance Pension schemes) which force citizens to contribute to a pension plan which would ensure a pension on retirement.

The Importance of Investing

Investment is the act of committing money or capital to an endeavor with the expectation of obtaining an additional income or profit. Investment is important to secure future income, plan for retirement, and cater for levels of inflation. If you become a millionaire before you reach 30 years but lose all of it by 40, you have not gained anything. If you grow and protect your investment portfolio carefully, you may be funding many future generations. Individuals can invest in a range of financial products such as bonds, stocks, annuity, mutual funds, a fixed deposit, treasury bills, and money market funds.

A Review of Investment in Financial Instruments

1. **Bonds:** This is a long-term instrument whose main purpose usually is to raise money or to provide capital to finance a project. Bonds are debt instruments issued by a government or company, which represents a fixed sum of money that was borrowed (principal). The issuer (borrower) promises to pay the holder (lender) a particular amount of interest (usually stated as a percentage) over a specified period of time and to repay the principal at maturity. Given that bondholders are usually paid before stockholders, this is viewed as a more secured investment option when compared to stocks. However, the rate of return on bonds is dependent on market conditions, normally a fixed coupon rate of interest.

2. **Shares or Stocks:** This is an equity investment that represents ownership in a company. There are two main types of shares, namely preferred and common. Although preferred shares is a form of equity (ownership) in a company, it is more a fixed-income investment because it pays a fixed dividend each year. Usually if a company is unable to make dividend payment to its preferred shareholders, the unpaid dividend accumulates and is paid in the following year and this type of shares is termed Cumulative Preference Shares. Preferred shareholders are paid dividends before common share holders. Their dividends are usually paid annually and are based on a percentage of par value. The par value of a share or is the issue price of the share or stock and has nothing to do with the market value of the stock.

   Common stockholders are the most popular class of equity which give their owners a residual claim on the assets and income of a business. This also means shareholders are entitled to all the earnings and assets of the company after the preferred shareholder's claims. Publicly quoted common share value is determined by demand and supply, and prices tend to fluctuate widely. Companies pay out a large portion of each year's profits to common shareholders (West Indies Tobacco Company Limited—WITCO) while others retain most of their income for reinvestment in the company with the shareholder hopefully benefitting from capital appreciation of stock. Common stockholders are able to elect the Board of Directors and thereby exercise some control over the company. Dividends are paid as a percentage of company's earnings and are normally paid quarterly, semi-annualy or annually. However, dividends are not guaranteed as common shareholders assume the primary risk if business is poor. Therefore, investors can lose their entire investment if the company fails.
3. **Annuity:** This is a contract between the investor and an insurance company, under which the investor makes a lump-sum payment or series of payments. In return, the insurer agrees to make periodic payments to the investor immediately upon retirement or at some other future agreed date. Annuities typically offer tax-deferred growth of earnings and may include a death benefit that will pay the beneficiary a guaranteed minimum amount.

4. **Mutual Funds:** This is an investment company that sells and repurchases shares/units. Equity-based mutual funds are those in which the underlying investments are primarily backed by equities. The value of the investment is subject to price movements of the underlying securities. Like all equity-based instruments, there are inherent risks of capital loss due to changes in the price of shares/stock.
5. **A fixed deposit:** Also referred to as a time deposit or a certificate of deposit (CD), a fixed deposit is basically a savings account that pays interest at rates higher than regular savings account but imposes conditions on the amount and period of withdrawal. Early encashment or of these funds imposes severe penalties.
6. **Treasury bills:** They are short-term, government-issued debt instruments available for purchase by any individual or company. There are variations in the return on issues because of the different maturity dates.
7. **A money market fund:** It is a very special type of mutual fund that is mandated to engage in short-term investments in low-risk securities. Compared to other mutual funds, they pay dividends on a short-term basis. Investment in a money market fund preserves your principal, that is, your initial investment, while yielding a modest return.
8. **Entrepreneurial pursuits:** Property, land, and business ventures are some of the avenues that can be explored as investment options. Rental of buildings, apartments, and houses can prove to be continuous sources of earnings to the investor. Additionally, proceeds from alternative business ventures or sale of land and property can provide a reasonable lump sum that can be utilized as capital for other investments. Senior entrepreneurship provides a further opportunity to the "retiree" to become an entrepreneur even after formal retirement.

Based on the discussions of the various instruments, it is clear that there is a direct/positive correlation between risk and return. In other words, the higher the risk of investing in a financial product, the higher the returns are likely to be from that financial instrument. This suggests that one has to assume certain risks and should be compensated accordingly.

Buying and Selling Stock

The Trinidad and Tobago Stock Exchange (TTSE) Limited is the nation's centralized marketplace for the buying and selling of shares or stocks and other securities. In addition to increasing the investment options available to individuals, the TTSE also provides a mechanism through which companies can raise capital for expansion purposes by issuing stocks and bonds.

To purchase shares you must visit a stock broker and open an account with them as well as with the Trinidad and Tobago Central Depository (TTCD). The stockbroker must be registered with the Securities and Exchange Commission (SEC) and licensed by the TTSE. To open an account with the TTCD, an investor will need two valid forms of identification and must sign a client agreement form with the stockbroker. The shares are issued by the company listed on the Exchange and are made available to the investing public. There is no minimum number of shares that an investor may purchase on the Exchange.

The Central Depository was established by the TTSE to facilitate the clearing and settlement of trades executed on the Exchange through a computerized book entry system. The computerized book entry system is an accounting system which aids the change of ownership of shares electronically between buyers and sellers without the need for the exchange of physical certificates. The settlement of transactions through the actual delivery of certificates was not always efficient. Additionally, there was the possibility that certificates could get lost, misplaced, stolen, or destroyed which would delay the process of transferring ownership.

The TTCD facilitates safe and efficient clearing and settlement of transactions. The use of the Depository also makes the settlement process more cost effective. The TTSE uses an electronic trading system which is tightly coupled with the inventory system of the TTCD to provide a smooth trading and settlement process. A trade can only be executed on the Exchange if the shares are available in the TTCD's inventory system. Shares will not be available for trading if they are pledged.

In light of the above a current shareholder with physical stock certificates desirous of selling, would need to lodge the stock certificates with the stockbroker to have them deposited in the TTCD. These shares are registered in the name of the TTCD and held on behalf of investors, so the investors maintain all their entitlements. Shares purchased will be credited to the investor's TTCD account. Payment for shares purchased should be made on or before settlement date whereas payment for shares sold will be received after settlement date. The settlement date is three business days after the trade date, the date on which the purchase or sale was made on your behalf.

After the broker has purchased or sold shares on your behalf, you will receive a contract note which is a legal document that specifies the volume and value of shares bought or sold, the transaction price, the Stock Exchange transaction charge, and the commission payable to the broker. In the case of a purchase, the contract note is your proof of legal ownership until the settlement date.

When a stockbroker sells shares on the Exchange, the TTCD will record the sale by reducing the balance of shares held in the seller's account by the number of shares sold and by simultaneously increasing the balance of shares held in the buyer's account. On settlement day (trade day plus three days), legal ownership is automatically transferred from the seller to the buyer.

Table 3.1 demonstrates that it takes considerably less time to trade in a non-certificated environment versus a certificated environment as there is a delay in lodging the share certificates prior to the sale of shares (certified environment).

The benefits of a non-certificated environment include the following:

- Facilitates easy and efficient transfer of ownership when a trade is completed. Immediately after a trade, the buyer's account is increased and the seller's account is reduced by the number of shares traded.

Table 3.1 Share certificated environment versus non-certificated environment

Certificated environment	VS	Non-certificated environment
Stock certificate must be deposited in the TTCD ↓ Three days to validate certificate and approve deposit ↓ Place order with broker to sell shares		Place order with broker to sell shares

- Ownership records are held in safekeeping electronically and there is no need to worry about lost certificates.
- Shares can be pledged as collateral for credit obligations at various financial institutions.

TTCD Statement

A quarterly statement is issued by the TTCD that reflects shares owned by investors in their TTCD accounts as well as any transactions such as purchases, sales, deposits, and pledges executed during the quarter. Stockbrokers are also required to send out periodic statements to their clients. The following is a typical TTCD statement.

Account Number, Broker (Member), Date Range of Statement

XYZ holdings	Owned	Available	Pledge
Opening balance	2000	1000	1000
Trade data (regular buy)	0		0
Trade data (set buy)	100	100	0
Closing balance	2100	1100	1000
Price: 4.00		Total value: $8400	

The statement is interpreted as follows:

Owned: The total shares held per security (available + pledged): 2100 shares

Available: The number of shares available for trade or transfer; the total number of shares owned less the number of shares pledged: 2100 – 1000 = 1100 shares

Pledge: The number of shares held as collateral for a loan facility (unavailable)—1000 shares.

Price: Price of the security as at statement date.

Value: Number of Shares × Price: 2100 x $4.00 = $8,400

Types of Transactions

- **Deposits**: Certificates deposited via a stockbroker are recorded as an electronic entry in a TTCD account. To deposit your share certificates, visit a stockbroker with your certificates and two valid forms of identification. An account will be created in the TTCD and your certificate will be deposited into your account.
- **Withdrawals**: Where a request is made for Shares to be removed from the TTCD a certificate is issued by the registrar of the listed company to the shareholder.
- **Inter-/Intra-member movements**: Movement of shares from one account to another with the same stockbroker or from an account with one stockbroker to an account **with another stockbroker**
- **Pledges**: Albeit shares are lodged with the TTCD shares can be used as collateral via the TTCD to financial institutions for credit/loan facilities
- **Cross-border transfers**: Shares can be transferred between the depositories in Trinidad, Jamaica, Barbados, or Eastern Caribbean for trading or safekeeping purposes.
- **Corporate actions**: Investors receive all correspondence and payments directly from the individual companies in which they have investments. Entitlements for shares lodged with the TTCD are distributed to investors, for example dividends and bonus or rights issues.
- **Registrar services**: The TTCD also provides registrar services for companies and facilitates transactions for shareholders who have not deposited their shares (physical certificates) with the TTCD.

TTCD Registrar Department

The TTCD Limited has established a Registrar Department that offers transfer agent and registrar services. The TTCD maintains the register of shareholders, processes stock transfers, and addresses inquiries from shareholders, brokers, and clearing agents.

Types of Transactions

Choosing the right broker is extremely important. The TTCD prides itself in being able to provide efficient and effective service to its customers. Some of these services rendered by the TTCD includes:

- Transfer and transaction inquiries,
- Processing and reissuance of lost share certificates,
- Confirmation/reporting/estate inquiries,
- Certificate issuance and/or cancelation,
- Shareholder information and updates,
- Dispatch of reports, accounts, and notices of Annual General Meetings (AGM) to shareholders,
- Preparation and registration for AGM,
- Preparation and filing of Annual Returns with the Registrar of Companies,
- Execution of corporate actions such as share issues, bonus issues, rights issues, dividend, and so on,
- Quick and efficient responses to queries and processes, and
- Reconciliation of dividends previously paid.

TTCD Registrar Requirements

There are different activities you can undertake at the TTCD Registrar Department and the Registrar, and the requirements for each are as follows:

1. Name change
    - Deed poll or marriage certificate or divorce document
    - Photo identification
2. Address change
    - Photo identification
    - Utility bill (showing new address, not necessarily in customer's name)

3. Direct deposit to bank account

    - Photo identification
    - Name of bank, address of bank, bank account number

4. Lost certificate

    - Indemnity form completed by shareholder and witnessed by a Commissioner of Affidavits
    - Photo identification
    - Receipt from daily newspaper for publishing lost certificate information for one day
    - Signed instructions from the shareholder or bondholder must be submitted with requests for the transactions listed above.

5. In the event that the any of the above transactions are being conducted on behalf of the shareholder, the following documents are also required:

    a. Letters of administration/grant of probate (in the case of a deceased shareholder)
    b. Power of Attorney (in the absence of the shareholder)
    c. Death certificate (if account is jointly held and one shareholder is deceased)

        - All documents presented must be originals and copies must be signed and certified by a Commissioner of Affidavits or notary public as being a true copy of the original.

6. Shareholders based outside of Trinidad and Tobago must submit notarized documents.
7. Deceased shareholder (single ownership)

    a. Original share certificates
    b. Original letters of administration/grant of probate
    c. Photo identification
    d. Stock transfer form (to be signed by executor)

        - Only executors can transfer shares.

8. Deceased shareholder (joint ownership)

   a. Original share certificates
   b. Original death certificate
   c. Photo identification
   d. Stock transfer form (to be signed by survivor)

      - Only the surviving party can transfer shares.

9. Converting joint ownership to single

   a. Original share certificates
   b. Photo identification of both parties
   c. Stock transfer form (to be signed by both parties)
   d. Statutory declaration witnessed by Commissioner of Affidavits requesting change of ownership
   e. Evidence that stamp duty has been paid

10. Converting single ownership to joint (must be 18 years and over)

    a. Original share certificate
    b. Photo identification of single owner
    c. Stock transfer form (to be signed by owner)
    d. Statutory declaration witnessed by Commissioner of Affidavits requesting joint transfer
    e. Evidence that stamp duty has been paid

11. As a gift

    a. Original share certificate
    b. Photo identification
    c. Stock transfer form
    d. Statutory declaration witnessed by Commissioner of Affidavits requesting transfer
    e. Evidence that stamp duty has been paid

Currently the TTCD Limited acts as Registrar for the following companies listed on the Trinidad and Tobago Stock Exchange:

- Republic Bank Limited
- Scotiabank of Trinidad and Tobago Limited

- National Flour Mills Limited
- Prestige Holdings Limited
- One Caribbean Media Limited
- Angostura Holdings Limited
- Trinidad Cement Limited
- Readymix (WI) Limited
- PLIPDECO Limited

The TTCD is also the Sub-registrar for the following:

- Sagicor Financial Corporation (Barbados)
- BCB Holdings Limited (Belize)
- GraceKennedy Limited (Jamaica)

The following is a list of stockbrokers and traders operating in Trinidad and Tobago:

- AIC Securities Limited
- Bourse Brokers Limited
- Caribbean Stockbrokers Limited
- First Citizens Brokerage & Advisory Services Limited
- Scotia Investments Trinidad & Tobago Limited
- Republic Securities Limited
- West Indies Stockbrokers Limited

Trading on the Stock Exchange

An investor can buy and sell shares on trading days. At the Stock Exchange trading takes place on all business days, excluding public holidays and carnival Monday and Tuesday from 9:30 am to 12:00 pm. The settlement period is three business days after the trade date.

Shares are an integral part of an individual's or company's investment portfolio. Investors in the local stock market have the opportunity to own shares in some of the largest and most profitable companies in the country and in the region. Shares provide investors with the opportunity to earn extra income from dividends which are paid out of the profits of a company and an opportunity for wealth accumulation on the appreciation of the price of shares. It can also be used as collateral to obtain loans from financial institutions.

On the other hand, if the share price falls, the investor suffers an unrealized loss and conversely enjoys an unrealized gain when the share price increases. Gains or losses are only realized when the shares are sold. Anyone can track the performance of the stock market by reviewing the Daily Trading Summary, which is published in the daily newspapers and can also be accessed on the website of the Stock Exchange. Interested individuals can also subscribe to receive the trading summaries via e-mail at the end of every trading day. Only the shares of companies registered with the SEC and listed on the Stock Exchange and can be bought or sold on the Exchange. This means that a company wishing to make its stocks available for trading must meet the listing requirements of the Exchange, which are a set of pre-determined standards.

You can have more than one stockbroker and if you have a complaint against your stockbroker, you can submit the complaint in writing to the Chief Executive Officer of the TTSE.

Initial Public Offering (IPO)

When a company wants to sell shares to the general public for the first time, it conducts an Initial Public Offering (IPO). By doing so, a company goes from the status of private (no general shareholders) to public (a firm with general shareholders). Private companies can have shareholders, but they are few in number and are not subject to regulations by the Securities and Exchange Commission. This changes dramatically with an IPO. An IPO usually takes three to four months from the beginning to the first day's trading on an exchange.

For fast-growing private companies seeking to raise capital, an IPO can be a superior route to fund growth and expansiion. An IPO is the first sale of a company's shares to the public and the listing of the shares on a stock exchange. It allows a company to raise capital to build its business by creating and selling new shares. Whereas not all businesses are suited to life in the public eye, many fast-growing private companies can become publicly quoted by issuing an IPO to raise the capital they need to accelerate growth and achieve market leadership.

A company can decide to go public for several reasons, but the raising of capital is a major consideration. It raises funds and the company has more liquidity or cash on hand by selling shares publicly. The money can be used in various ways, such as reinvesting in the company's infrastructure or expanding the business. An added benefit from issuing shares is that they can be used to attract top management candidates through the offer of benefits or perks like stock option plans. In addition there are several advantages that a limited liability company enjoys versus a private company. Another advantage of going public is that shares/stocks can be used in merger and acquisition deals as part of the payment. Being listed on a reputable stock exchange can create many opportunities and lower the cost of borrowing money in the market. There's also the prestige, bragging rights for some firms, of being listed on a major stock exchange like the NYSE or NASDAQ.

A firm going public hires an investment bank, or banks, to handle the IPO. It is possible for a company to sell shares on its own, but this can be risky if the offer is not deemed attractive and not fully subscribed. Investment banks can work alone or together on one IPO, with one taking the lead. They usually form a group of banks or investors to spread around the funding and the risk for the IPO. Banks submit bids to companies going public on how much money the firm will make in the IPO and what the bank will walk away with. The process of an investment bank handling an IPO is called underwriting.

When an investment bank, is eventually hired, the company and the investment bank negotiate the amount of money they will raise from the IPO, the type of securities to be issued, and all the other details in the underwriting agreement.

After the company and investment bank agree to an underwriting deal, the bank puts together a registration statement to be filed with the Trinidad and Tobago Security Exchange Commission (SEC). This statement has detailed information about the offering and company information such as financial statements, management background, any legal problems, where the money is to be used, and who owns any stock before the company goes public. The SEC, as the regulator will investigate the company to make sure all the information contained in an IPO is correct and that all relevant financial data have been disclosed. If everything is in order, the SEC will work with the company to set a date for the IPO. After SEC approves the IPO, the underwriter must put together a prospectus, that is, all financial information of the company which includes the last five year audited financial statements.

A bank or group of banks put up the money to fund the IPO and "buy" the shares of the company before they are actually listed on a stock exchange. The banks make their profit on the difference in price between what they paid before the IPO and when the shares are officially offered to the public. Competition among investment banks for handling an IPO can be fierce, depending on the company that's going public and the money the bank thinks it will make on the deal.

To raise interest in the IPO, the underwriter takes the prospectus and presents it to prospective investors. This is called a road show. These can be trips around the world, thus the name road show, or can be video or Internet presentations. If a prospective investor likes the IPO, underwriters can legally offer them shares at the price they eventually set before the stock is listed on an exchange. This is called IPO allocation. Road shows are usually for the bigger institutional investors like pension funds rather than an individual investor.

Like underwriters, stock exchanges such as the NASDAQ and NYSE want the business of an IPO. There is also the prestige of having a famous company listed. Exchanges make representations to the companies, and then the underwriting firm will make the final selection. In Trinidad and Tobago Stock Exchange, the companies listed in the Small and Medium Enterprise (SME) Market category enjoy a preferential rate of corporation tax of 10%.

When a firm goes public, it legally falls under the guidelines of the SEC. This includes disclosure rules like holdings and transactions of insiders or the officers and directors of the company, publish of financial statements on a periodic basis and come under surveillance by the SEC on its trading practices. It will have to hold regular shareholders' meetings. It should recognize the need for enhanced corporate governance, especially recruiting qualified non-executive board members, improving internal controls, and forming sub committees of the board including a qualified audit committee. It must deal with current accounting challenges, especially asset valuation impairment, consolidated subsidiary financial statement issues, and revenue recognition.

The IPO process should be a structured and managed transformation of the people, processes, and culture of an organization. This process is referred to as the IPO value journey. Although the IPO event itself generally lasts 90 to 120 days, the value journey begins at least a year or two before the IPO and continues well beyond it. While an IPO should be a key turning point in the life of a company, market leaders do not treat an IPO as simply a one-time financial transaction. They recognize the IPO event itself as just one defining milestone in a complex transformation from a private to a public company.

The IPO value journey occurs via the following phases:

- IPO planning phase,
- IPO execution phase,
- IPO realization phase, and
- Life as a public company

Secrets of highly successful IPOs:

- Prepare early and begin the IPO process early so that the prelisted company acts and operates like a public company at least a year before the IPO.
- Commit substantial resources to the IPO process and build a quality management team, robust financial and business infrastructure, and corporate governance and investor relations strategy that will attract the right investors.
- Properly assess the amount of time the IPO journey and prepare for the increased level of scrutiny and accountability faced by a public company.

Outperform Competitors on Key Benchmarks

- Investors generally base an average of 60% of their IPO investment decisions on financial factors especially debt-to-equity ratios, Earnings Per Share (EPS) growth, sales growth, Return on Investment (ROE), profitability and Earnings before Interest, Tax, Depreciation and Amortization (EBITDA).

- Investors base about 40% of their IPO investment decisions on non-financial factors especially quality of management, corporate strategy and execution, brand strength and operational effectiveness, and corporate governance
- Articulate a compelling equity story backed up by a strong track record of growth, which sets the company apart from its peers while maximizing value for owners.

Evaluate Options for Sourcing of Capital

When evaluating capital-raising options a company should consider a "multitrack approach." The expanding number of capital-raising strategies include a strategic sale to a trade or financial buyer; joint venture; private placement; or a foreign listing. Pursue pre-IPO transactions to achieve maximum value, especially debt financing and refinancing, corporate reorganization, private placements, or business alliances.

Type of Information Needed to Make an Investment Decision

Shares or stocks should be selected through the process of investment analysis and portfolio management—functions which can be performed by a stockbroker. If you have a large investment portfolio, you may want to develop an investment policy to ensure optimization of returns and diversification of risks. Investment analysis takes into consideration the financial policies of a company, the sources of its growth, the ability of its management team, and the investment quality of its stocks. From this appraisal, stocks are then analyzed in the larger context of the economy. Then an investment portfolio or mix of different stocks is selected which best fits the needs, objectives, and risk tolerance of each investor.

Here are some of the financial ratios you would consider when purchasing shares.

Earnings Per Share (EPS)

This is the net income (after preference dividend) divided by the number of outstanding ordinary shares.

It should be noted that when a company has preferred stock, the dividend due to preferred shareholders is deducted first. For example, assume a company has Net Income of $1,500,000 and outstanding share capital of 1,000,000 shares.

The Earnings per Share is calculated as follows:

Net Income = $1,500,000
Dividends on Preferred stock = $480,000
Applicable to Ordinary stock = $1,020,000 ($1,500,000-$480,000)
EPS = $1,020,000/ 1,000,000 (Net income after dividend payments/ No of issued shares)
= $1.02

Price Earnings Ratio (P/E)

This is the share price of an ordinary share divided by the earnings per share. The P/E is sometimes referred to as the "multiple," because it shows how much investors are willing to pay per dollar of earnings. P/E ratios are useful to compare companies in the same industry, the overall market, or the company's historical P/E ratio.

The P/E ratio is calculated as follows:

Share price per ordinary share = $10.00
Earnings per share = $2.00
Price Earnings Ratio (P/E) = $10.00 /$2.00 (Price/ Earnings per Share)
= 5

Investors use the price-to-earnings **ratio** (P/E **ratio** or price multiple) to evaluatae whether a company's stock price is over- or undervalued.

Companies with a high P/E **ratio** are typically growth stocks. The price earnings ratio, often called the P/E ratio or price-to-earnings ratio, is a market prospect ratio that calculates the market value of a stock relative to its earnings by dividing the market price per share by the earnings per share. The P/E ratio shows what the market is willing to pay for a stock, the price being a multiple of the current earnings per share. Investors often use this ratio to evaluate what a stock's fair market value should be by predicting future earnings per share. Companies with higher future earnings are usually expected to issue higher dividends or have appreciating stock in the future. Investor speculation and demand also help increase a share's price over time.

Dividend Yield

This is the annual dividend payments divided by the share price and is usually expressed as a percentage. The dividend yield is calculated as follows:

Annual Dividends = $0.50
Share price = $5.00
Dividend Yield = $0.50/$5.00
= 0.10 or 10%

Understanding Issues and Transactions in the Financial Sector

- Cheques are generally held by the financial institutions for four working days to check for any inconsistencies, such as, words and figures not matching; incorrect date; stale dated or postdated. If any of these inconsistencies are found, the cheque is returned to the person who deposited the check. The bank also verifies to see if there are sufficient funds to cover the cheque and the authenticity of the signature before releasing the funds.
- It is a criminal offense to write a cheque for an amount greater than what is available in your account; in other words the inability to honor a cheque amounts to a criminal offense.

- Businesses and individuals should retain financial records for six years. Financial records include account statements; loan, hire purchase, and mortgage contracts; and filed tax forms, and tax statements.
- Banks retain financial records for ten years. Check your account statements as soon as you get them. Query abnormalities and odd bank charges immediately. The less time lapse between the issue of the statement and the query the faster and easier the bank will deal with your query.
- Do not overextend yourself; loan payments should be comfortable to make and within the acceptable debt to income ratio of 35–40%
- Refinance or consolidate debt if necessary.
- Keep a savings account separate from your main account. The former will provide an emergency fund.

4

Debt Management

Effective Management of Debt

Debt management is the systematic way to manage the payment of outstanding debt and involves working with creditors and refinancing of loans. There are a variety of practices that make it difficult to manage debt effectively. These include spending more than you have, impulse purchases, buying things you do not need, using credit when you have cash, and refusing to budget wisely.

Individuals can undertake a variety of measures to ensure they manage debt effectively. They can negotiate with creditors, engage in better money management, and seek to build their overall credit ratings. There are a variety of signs that are indicative of debt trouble such as when an individual's credit card balances are rising while income is decreasing; paying only the minimum amounts required on accounts or maybe even less than the minimum, and juggling of bills. For example, if someone applies for another credit card and uses cash advances from it to pay an existing card.

C. Sahadeo, *Financial Literacy and Money Script*,
https://doi.org/10.1007/978-3-319-77075-8_4

Debt trouble is also visible when: an individual has several credit cards or is at or perilously near the limit on credit cards; is consistently charged more each month than actual payments; is working overtime to keep up with credit card payments; does not know how much is owed to third parties and really does not want to find out the extent of his debt.

Other signs of ineffective credit card debt management include:

1. Using credit cards not for the sake of convenience but to get credit because you have no money,
2. Dipping into savings, emergency fund or your retirement account to pay monthly bills,
3. Hiding the true cost of purchases from your spouse,
4. Playing the card game by signing up for every credit card that sends you an unsolicited offer.

Why Do People Borrow?

Individuals may borrow money in order to purchase capital items. Some reasons for borrowing include: to purchase a car or home, to pay for their education, to take a vacation, or to invest in a business (entrepreneurship). Nevertheless, it is noteworthy that borrowing usually differs at various stages of the family life cycle. Please refer to Fig. 4.1.

Financial institutions compute a debt-to-income ratio for all prospective borrowers whereby a ratio in excess of 40% would disqualify the borrower. Debt-to-income ratio can be calculated using this simple worksheet:

Minimum monthly credit card payment ....
+ Monthly car loan payment ....
+ Other monthly debt payment ....
+ Expected mortgage payment ....
= Total monthly payments ....

Your debt-to-income ratio:

Total monthly payments/gross income = ...

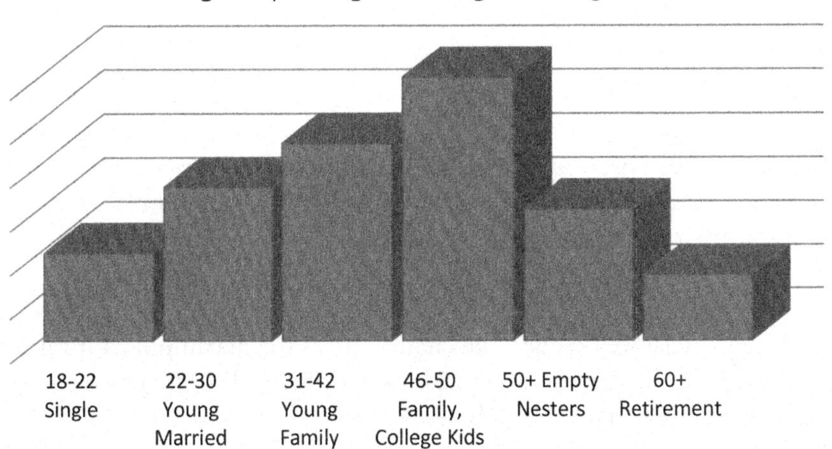

Fig. 4.1 Borrowing at the various stages of the family life cycle

Main Types of Credit

The main types of credit available to an individual are loans, installment/hire purchase credit, and credit cards.

1. Loans: This is a sum of money that is borrowed usually from a financial institution such as a commercial bank or credit union that is expected to be paid back in installments which includes the principal sum borrowed and interest. The payment is usually made in monthly installments, and collateral or security is generally held against the loan. Collateral is something of worth which the financial institution can take possession of and sell to recoup any outstanding amount on the loan that an individual is unable to pay. This may include mortgage and mortgage bill of sale.
2. Installment/Hire purchase credit: This is an arrangement whereby a person pays for an item via monthly installments. The purchaser has use of the item but gets actual ownership only after all installments have been made. Interest charges are added to the cash price and the installment is then computed by dividing by the number of months for which the credit is granted. A hire purchase agreement is the con-

tract that binds the purchaser and the company until all intallments are paid.

3. Credit card: A credit card is a means of executing payment by drawing on a line of credit up to an agred limit with a financial institution that issued the card. This form of payment mechanism is becoming more common as a way of conducting transactions. However, there are many characteristics of a credit card such as credit limit, balance, annual percentage rate (APR), grace period, finance charge, incentives and rewards, and credit card fees.

   Financial institutions give cardholders a credit limit depending on their financial well-being. The credit limit is the maximum cash value assigned to the card by the financial institution. This credit limit can be for cash advances or purchases. Holders of the card are not allowed to charge payments or withdrawals in excess of the assigned limit on their card, even if the holder has funds in the current account. However the balance can be paid during the grace period to facilitate credit card transactions thereafter.

   The balance on the credit card is the amount of credit the cardholder has used since the last reimbursement of the credit card balance. It is the total of cash advances, purchases, and credit card fees.

Finance and Other Charges

The finance charge is the cost of carrying an outstanding balance. Finance charges are computed using the balance, the APR, and the time the balance is deemed to be outstanding in respect of the grace period. Some credit cards carry a minimum finance charge. If the calculated finance charge is less than the minimum, one must still pay the minimum charge. Some of the most common fees are annual fees, finance charges, late fees, and over-the-limit fees. The APR is the interest rate applied to a balance carried beyond the grace period. Cash advances usually have higher APRs than purchases and there is automatic immediate charge to your credit card for cash withdrawal.

Grace Period

This is the amount of time granted to pay the outstanding balance in full after which charges are applied. If a balance is brought forward from a previous month, additional purchases may not qualify for the grace period. Cash advances generally do not have a grace period. To find out the length of the grace period, you should refer to the credit card application or your credit card agreement.

Incentives and Rewards

Many credit cards offer incentives and rewards for using the card. Different cards offer different rewards, for example a money back coupon that can be cashed at particular stores. The value of the coupon will be determined by the amount of money charged to the card (the more money charged the higher the value of the coupon). Another example is getting back airline miles which can then be used to purchase airline tickets or upgrade your ticket.

What to Consider When Choosing a Credit Card?

- Your personal spending habits,
- The purposes for which the card is to be used,
- The pre-approved credit limit that you will be granted,
- The length of the grace period, if any,
- The interest rate applied to unpaid balances and all associated charges,
- All the terms and conditions of using the card,
- The extent of local, regional, or international acceptability of the card for which you are applying, and
- The incentives and reward.

There are numerous advantages and disadvantages that can arise from using credit cards. This financial tool is considered convenient: it eliminates the need to carry large sums of cash, provides additional purchasing power, and provides various incentives such as bonus points, discounts, and cashback rewards, and travel miles are offered with usage of these cards. On the other hand, credit cards carry high interest charges. If credit card accounts are not paid off in full on or before the due date, these charges can be as high as 2% per month or 24% per annum. The interest charged for late payment of these accounts is often the main reason for the accumulation of credit card debts.

Credit card debt arises when the outstanding balance is not paid off in full on or before the due date and mainly results from agreed minimum payments instead of full settlement of the outstanding balance. This minimum payment option is often the main cause of customers getting into insurmountable credit card debt. When balances are left unsettled, interest charges accrue thus increasing the amount to be repaid.

There are numerous strategies that can be undertaken to avoid credit card debt. For example, individuals who cannot manage repayments should not use a credit card. Individuals should not accept an increase in their credit limit if their monthly income is inadequate to cover payment. To avoid this type of debt, individuals can also adopt the following strategies:

1. Pay the full outstanding balance on or before the due date. Avoid making only the minimum payments on the credit card.
2. Avoid having too many credit cards.
3. Shop around for the credit card that best suits your individual needs, ensuring that you compare interest rates, administration fees, acceptability by the merchants you patronize, and the interest-free periods for repayment.
4. Avoid withdrawing cash through your credit card as this attracts additional charges.

Prevention of Credit Card Fraud

Credit card fraud refers to the unauthorized use of a credit card to make purchases or obtain funds from someone else's account. You should take the following steps to avoid credit card fraud.

- Never disclose your Personal Identification Number (PIN) to anyone.
- Refrain from writing down and/or leaving your PIN in a conspicuous place.
- Keep your card with you at all times and in a safe place.
- Always keep your credit card in your view; when you are doing transactions with your credit card you have a right to observe.
- Draw a line through any space above your total when signing your credit card receipt.
- Report lost or stolen credit card immediately to the bank in order to minimize unauthorized transactions.
- Always reconcile your credit card statements quickly and query any charges that you do not know about.
- Never disclose your credit card information over the phone or in an e-mail. When talking to individuals on the phone claiming to be from your credit card company, exercise caution and be sure they are who they say they are before disclosing information.

Strategies to maintain and build a good credit rating include the following:

- Pay all bills on time including your credit card bill, utilities bill, any loan or hire purchase payments. which can be done by setting up standing orders for automatic payments of bills or use an electronic device to provide reminders of when different payments become due.
- Do not carry a high balance on your credit card.
- Do not take out additional credit cards.
- Apply for new credit accounts only as needed.

- Protect your credit information by not sharing your credit card information or PIN numbers on the telephone or via e-mails. If you become a victim of fraud or identity theft, it will negatively impact your credit rating.

What Is a Debit Card?

A debit card, sometimes referred to as an Automated Teller Machine (ATM) card, is a widely accepted payment instrument. This accounts for almost a third of non-cash payments in Trinidad and Tobago. This card enables the holder to have his/her purchases directly charged to funds on his/her account and also facilitates the withdrawal of cash from ATM machines. Therefore, unlike a credit card, these cards allow users to access their own funds. These cards may be internationally or locally branded and can be used to pay for everyday items such as groceries, meals, and shopping.

Each financial institution sets a predetermined limit to values at both Point of Sale (POS) and ATM withdrawals. This is deemed a safety measure and protects the cardholder. For example, certain banks have a limit of $5000 and ATM withdrawal is $2500. Some financial institutions charge a fee for using ATM machines at any of their outlets, whether at a branch or facility (e.g., gas station). However, all financial institutions charge a fee if you use your debit card at an outlet belonging to another financial institution.

If you have a TT-dollar, international debit card issued by a local bank, you can pay for purchases or withdraw cash from an ATM in a foreign country. The TT-dollar equivalent of the foreign currency amount will be withdrawn from your bank account. There is usually a higher charge for using your debit card to withdraw cash. This charge varies with each financial institution.

Credit and Debit Card Safety Tips

- *Keep your ATM/Debit card in a safe place* and never "lend" it to anyone, including friends and family members.
- *Keep your PIN private.* Your PIN is your Personal Identification Number. Memorize it and do not give it to anyone, even a bank employee.
- *Conduct ATM transactions* ***only*** *when and where you feel safe.*
- *Use your hand or body* as a shield to prevent others from observing the details of your transaction.
- *Remember to take your card and your transaction record* after completing your transaction.
- *Count the cash received and secure it immediately* after making a withdrawal.
- *Reconcile withdrawal slips and LINX* receipts against account statements on a regular basis.
- *Destroy and discard* withdrawal slips and LINX receipts after you have reconciled your statement as these slips contain confidential information.
- *Report any irregularity when doing an ATM transaction* to the account branch manager immediately. Keep the ATM receipt as supporting documentation to be shown to the manager.
- *Report lost or stolen cards* immediately to the financial institution.
- *Report any fraudulent use of your card* immediately to your financial institution.
- *Do not keep your PIN alongside your card.*
- *Do not choose a PIN that others can figure out* like birthdays and phone numbers.
- *Do not accept assistance from unknown people* at the ATM site.
- *Do not ask anyone to conduct your transaction* for you.

5

Planning for Retirement

Retirement Planning

Retirement is the stage in a person's life whereby they withdraw from their occupation, business, or office that is, they cease to be gainfully employed. Therefore, retirement planning is often referred to as the allocation and investment of funds for one's retirement. The goal is to achieve financial independence on retirement. Some other goals and objectives for retirement are to have adequate funds, staying healthy, enjoying a good quality of life, caring for dependents, traveling, and passing on wealth to others.

Importance of Planning for Retirement

Retirement from active employment requires planning and commitment. The planning process is very crucial and individuals should start this process as early as possible that is, from the time a person enters the world of work. The earlier one begins to fund their retirement needs, the higher the probability of his or her being financially better off in retirement.

C. Sahadeo, *Financial Literacy and Money Script*,
https://doi.org/10.1007/978-3-319-77075-8_5

A common mistake of many employed persons is the belief that they should begin thinking about retirement only when they have crossed the age of 40 or 50 years. On the contrary, planning for retirement must be identified as one of the critical financial goals that one must establish early in one's working life. This deliberate approach to preparation and provision for a retirement cannot be overemphasized. The earlier you begin to fund your retirement needs, the higher the probability of the adeqacy of the retirement fund.

Retirement planning is critical since individuals are now living many more years after they retire from active employment. Advancement in healthcare treatment and services has extended the life expectancy of individuals. Moreover, there are numerous social, psychological, and financial issues that are associated with this phase of life, which should ideally be addressed long before the assumption of "retiree" status. Therefore, it is important that workers take responsibility for making adequate provision for later years.

It is no longer safe to depend on a government pension as one's only source of retirement income. Societies are now facing a change in the age distribution of their population which is characterized by a growing aged population. Consequently, countries have started to promote investment in personal pension plans to relieve some of this retirement burden placed on their governments. Therefore, individuals who are not permanently employed should take the initiative to invest in a pension plan that will cater to their retirement needs.

Planning for Retirement

In recent times, many organizations have been encouraging new entrants into the work place to embark on a savings/investment program. These programs will generate a flow of additional income that would enable employees to augment their retirement benefits.

Several issues must be considered in undertaking a retirement planning program. It is important to protect yourself against the real risk of inflation on the value of funds over time. One of the ways of hedging or minimizing such risk is through prudent investment of funds. The instruments in which these funds are invested must ideally provide a rate of return that is superior to the rate of inflation. While in general, current rates of return on various investments may not be attractive to the simple investor, the level of risk of the investment must be a factor to be considered.

Another item to consider is to plan and budget expenses during one's working life so that you will not be unnecessarily burdened with huge expenses during retirement. For example, make the necessary adjustments while still actively employed, to ensure the outstanding mortgage balance is repaid prior to retirement. Also make adequate provision for health services during retirement to reduce the cost of health care when it is needed the most. One way of doing so is to become a member of a group or individual health plan that would provide coverage into retirement.

In the early years of financial planning, it is imperative that arrangements are made to ensure there are two or more sources of income during retirement. One test of adequacy of financial planning for retirement is the extent of diversification of investment and sources of income. A typical retirement portfolio may include any combination of the following instruments which carry varying degrees of risk:

- Fixed deposits and other savings plans,
- Treasury bills,
- Corporate and government bonds,
- Money market funds,
- Stocks and shares,
- Equity-based mutual funds,
- Annuities, and
- Entrepreneurial pursuits (real estate, small business, etc.).

It is important that the retirement fund is a balanced portfolio with a suitable asset mix, structured in accordance with one's financial situation, risk tolerance, length of time to retirement, as well as in sync with your financial goals. Providing for one's retirement has become particularly important for every worker, not only in Trinidad and Tobago, but the world over. This is largely because of the changes in the demographics of the population which has been taking place over the last five decades or so. One reason for such change is that today the life expectancy of the population is increasing and this is a trend that is evident not only in Trinidad and Tobago but around the world. Because people are living for many more years after their years of active employment, it is important that workers take responsibility for making adequate provision for the later years.

Evaluate the Adequacy of Employer's Pension on Retirement

While many employees may benefit from a company's pension plan the income from these arrangements are usually woefully inadequate for the individual to maintain an appropriate standard of living on retirement. In fact, it is unreasonable to expect an employer to fully provide for an employee after he/she has ended active service. Pension arrangements are meant to assist the employee during the period of retirement, but the responsibility for making adequate provision for one's post-employment years rests entirely with the individual.

One of the problems employees tend to have is the belief that they should only begin thinking about "retirement" when they have crossed the age of 40 or 50 years. In fact, more and more, new entrants into the workforce are encouraged to embark on a savings/investment program. This will generate regular income over a longer period to enable them to augment their retirement income.

To do this properly, one must begin to structure a financial plan early in one's working life, setting goals and targets over time with one major component being "savings for retirement." If this is done successfully, one can even retire voluntarily ahead of the official retirement age. Many persons have been able to do this, but it does not happen by chance. It must be carefully planned! As you approach your retirement, there are some questions that you need to ask yourself.

(i) At what age do I want to retire?
(ii) How do I maintain at least my current lifestyle after my retirement?
(iii) Given (ii) above, how much should I save now in order to meet these goals?

Your current age will determine how much time you have to amass your retirement fund. The size of the retirement fund or nest egg will determine the earning potential of the "retirement fund." Looking at some possible scenarios:

(a) At age 20 and a planned retirement age of say 55, there are 35 years or 420 monthly salaries to retirement.
(b) At age 30 and a planned retirement age of say 55, there are 25 years or 300 monthly salaries to retirement.
(c) At age 40 and a planned retirement age of say 55, there are 15 years or 180 monthly salaries to retirement.

In each of these possible scenarios if you use an average monthly contribution of say $1000.00 the total savings (before interest) will be as follows:

(a) At age 20 and a planned retirement age of say 55 = $420,000.
(b) At age 30 and a planned retirement age of say 55 = $300,000.
(c) At age 40 and a planned retirement age of say 55 = $180,000.

If you use an average monthly contribution of say $500.00 the total savings (before interest) will be as follows:

(d) At age 20 and a planned retirement age of say 55 = $210,000.
(e) At age 30 and a planned retirement age of say 55 = $150,000.
(f) At age 40 and a planned retirement age of say 55 = $90,000.

While if you use an average monthly contribution of say $100.00 the total savings (before interest) will be as follows:

(g) At age 20 and a planned retirement age of say 55 = $42,000.
(h) At age 30 and a planned retirement age of say 55 = $30,000.

(i) At age 40 and a planned retirement age of say 55 = $18,000.

The above clearly illustrates that ***the earlier we start to save and fund our retirement, the greater will be the retirement fund.***

There are some other considerations that must be taken into account when computing your retirement fund:

- The impact of inflation on the value of the "fund" and its earnings in say 15, 25, or 35 years can only be preserved by investing in instruments such as stocks and shares and equity-based mutual funds.
- Streamlining one's expenses during active employment years so that you will not be unnecessarily burdened with huge expenses such as mortgage payments when you go into retirement
- Make adequate provision for your health services during retirement, if possible. One way of doing so is to become a member of a group or individual health plan that would provide coverage into retirement.
- Do not depend on one source of income during retirement and hold investmesnts in a diversified portfolio.

Statistics Regarding Retired Persons in Trinidad and Tobago

- 11% of the population is over 60 years.
- The population is expected to grow to 20% by 2020.
- Life expectancy for males is 67.8 years and 71.8 years for females.
- According to the NFLP Survey on retirement planning:

1. Nearly 50% of retirees have no occupational pension.
2. Only 13% considered taking out a personal pension plan.
3. Almost 50% of retirees interviewed lived below the preretirement standard.
4. About 69% of respondents relied on NIS/Senior Citizens Grant.

In the UK, the population in 2016 was at its largest ever, at 65.6 million with 18% of people aged 65 and over, and 2.4% were aged 85 and over. Barbados has a population of 280,000 people and has the highest number of persons aged 65 and over in the English-speaking Caribbean with 11.3% of the population over 65 years. By and large the entire world now has aging populations with dire consequences regarding funding of pensions.

The risks on retirement are greater as the opportunity for income generation generally decreases on relinquishing one's job. Further many unforeseen expenses of the retiree or the immediate family can result in financial instability and even bankruptcy. The death of a spouse is extremely emotional and stressful and can result in substantial reduction in the income of the surviving partner. Divorce after retirement can result in hardship if there are inadequate pension arrangements.

Popular Myths About Retirement

There is a lot of false information that exists out there about retirement that can derail how you prepare for its eventuality. Here are some of the myths to avoid:

- You will die before money runs out.
- Expenses will go down.
- Your children will take care of you.
- Your company pension plan will be enough.
- Wait until midlife to start saving.

Main Sources of Retirement Income

The main sources of retirement income are the following:

1. Employer-sponsored pension,
2. Government/senior citizen pension,
3. Private pension plan,
4. National Insurance Pension,
5. Tax-deferred annuity income,
6. Non-registered annuity plans,

7. Investments—for example, shares, stocks,
8. Part-time or consulting employment income.

Factors That Determine the Level of Retirement Income

There are numerous factors that determine the level of retirement income. They are:

1. Current age,
2. Expected retirement age,
3. Expected years in retirement,
4. Current income,
5. Other retirement income,
6. Desired retirement income,
7. Current tax rate,
8. Rate of inflation,
9. Expected return on fund,

What Is a Retirement Fund?

A personal retirement fund refers to assets accumulated over a period of time identified and designated for use during retirement. Income from this fund is used to supplement employment retirement benefits.

A typical retirement fund, whether it is personal or group, can include any combination of the following instruments: (see Chap. 3)

(i) Fixed Deposits and Other Savings Plans
(ii) Treasury Bills
(iii) Corporate and Government Bonds
(iv) Money Market Funds
(v) Stocks and Shares
(vi) Equity-based Mutual Funds

(vii) Annuities
(viii) Entrepreneurial Pursuits (Real Estate, Small Business).

Planning and Budgeting

Budgeting continues to be important after retirement as the income received during retirement is usually considerably less than during active employment. Planning and budgeting will require having a clear understanding of the sources and amount of your income and expenses.

Making some lifestyle changes provides the opportunity to plan travel and try new things, and even relocate to a less expensive home or one that is easier to maintain.

Retirement Benefits in Trinidad and Tobago

As a retiree aged 60 years or older, you are entitled to a number of services provided by the government. It would be wise to take advantage of these facilities since they would help in reducing your expenses. In Trinidad and Tobago some of these benefits include old age pension, free bus pass, free access to Chronic Disease Assistance Program (CDAP).

National Insurance Board (NIB) Retirement Benefit

Every employee who has paid National Insurance contributions is entitled to a Retirement Benefit. You qualify for the Retirement Benefit at any time between the ages of 60 and 65 if you are retired, or at age 65 whether you are retired or not. The amount you receive depends on the number of contributions you have made.

Old Age Pension or Senior Citizens Grant

The Old Age Pension or Senior Citizens Grant is available to Senior Citizens 65 years of age and older whose monthly income is less than $2800.

Free Bus Pass

Senior Citizens can apply for a free bus pass, allowing them to travel freely on buses run by the Public Transport Service Corporation (PTSC).

Free Medical Care and Drugs

Citizens can access the CDAP. This program allows persons to receive free prescription drugs and other pharmaceutical items from designated CDAP pharmacies throughout Trinidad and Tobago. The program makes provisions for most illnesses that plague many senior citizens.

Retirement Benefits in Other Countries

Since 2003, Barbados has made several changes to its pension system to ensure that future generations receive an adequate pension. As a result of pension reform, the pensionable age has increased by six months every four years from January 1, 2006 until it reached 67 years on January 1, 2018. Barbados has also introduced a flexible retirement/pensionable age between 60 and 70.

In Jamaica, the reform of the public-sector pension system was born out of the recognition that the current system had become fiscally unsustainable thus rendering it unaffordable. Minister of State in the Ministry of Labour and Social Security, Andrew Gallimore, is advising unemployed persons, to contribute to the National Insurance Scheme (NIS). Mr. Gallimore said that currently, only about 33% of the senior citizens are receiving a pension benefit from the NIS, which means that roughly

66% of the senior citizens did not make plans for retirement. He said, "There are many senior citizens who are having it far more difficult than they should have or would have, if they had been proactively planning for their retirement."

Postponing or Delaying Retirement

More and more individuals are choosing to postpone retirement even though they have reached retirement age. Sometimes this is because they are not prepared financially for retirement, or sometimes it is simply because they feel fit and able to continue working. If you choose to continue working for a few more years on a full-time or part-time basis, you should try to save as much as you can for the time when you do retire. ***Remember, retirement is not the end of your life. It is really the beginning of a new stage of living!***

Organizations for Retirees

Two organizations which have been in existence for some time and whose membership is exclusive to retired persons are the Trinidad and Tobago Association of Retired Persons (TTARP) and the Government Pensioners Association of Trinidad and Tobago (GPATT).

The TTARP was established in 1993 and is open to all persons who have attained retiree status. One of its major functions is to leverage providers of goods and services for favorable terms and conditions for, and on behalf of, its membership. As a consequence, members of TTARP gain access to a wide range of services, usually at some very attractive discounts. Included among these services are banking, insurance, medical, pharmaceutical, dental, optical care, travel, supermarket, retail stores, and automotive care. In addition, the organization is engaged in social and cultural activities to facilitate recreation and camaraderie among retirees.

GPATT was established in 1957. Membership of GPATT is restricted to former employees of the government service who are recipients of government pension, as well as spouses of government pensioners. Its role is similar to TTARP's in that it is primarily engaged in lobbying with government, merchants, and other service providers for the benefit of its members. GPATT also has a social program for its members. Information on this organization can be obtained through the telephone contact: 662-4389.

Trade Unions and Retirees

Trade unions have also established a special category of membership for their retirees. Membership is normally offered at a minimal cost to the individual, although he/she continues to enjoy most of the benefits of an active member. Usually there is some qualification requirement, for example, minimum period of continuous membership, to be able to access facilities offered. However the extent of access and the range of facilities offered to retirees can vary from union to union and can even vary from unit to unit within the same trade union.

Employers and Retirees

In some other organizations, it is not uncommon for retirees to continue enjoying membership and benefits of their former employer's group medical plan, and if it exists, scholarship programs for children of staff. Some progressive employers have even gone as far as supporting the establishment of "Retirees Clubs" or "Retirees Associations" for their former employees. Within these clubs, programs aimed at developing activities of a social, welfare, or economic nature are organized and pursued.

Financial Products for Retirees

Many financial institutions, including commercial banks, insurance companies, credit unions, and mutual fund management companies have structured a full array of specially designed products and services geared toward satisfying the needs of senior citizens. Generally, eligibility for these services commences at the age of 50. In addition to the products offered, services provided by these institutions include:

- Discounts at a wide range of merchants,
- Advice on will preparation, and
- Waiving of credit card fees, and other service charges.

The foregoing gives a broad spectrum of services which are available to retirees.

6

Risk Management

Risk management is the process of identifying risk and then finding ways to avoid or minimize their impact. Insurance is one of the most useful tools for protecting yourself from risk. Insurance can help you manage the risk of relatively rare but expensive events throughout your life such as car accident, theft, or fire. Without the protection of an insurance policy, you would be responsible for covering the loss you have experienced.

Types of Insurance

There are various types of insurance namely deposit insurance, life insurance, and general insurance. Deposit insurance provides protection to people who have deposited money in any one of the licensed financial institutions. Life insurance pays money to the insured or their beneficiaries under particular circumstances, that is, after a specified period, death, or permanent disability. The major products of life insurance include whole life, endowment, term, and investment-linked. This type of insurance is particularly important to protect the family of the main bread winner in the household. It also protects the

C. Sahadeo, *Financial Literacy and Money Script*,
https://doi.org/10.1007/978-3-319-77075-8_6

main bread winner from illness and provides income during retirement.

General insurance on the other hand protects you from losses and damages not covered by life insurance, for example home insurance, motor insurance, creditor insurance, travel insurance, and so on. Under General Insurance there is a commercial line of products for businesses, such as employer liability, public liability, product liability, and so on.

Deposit Insurance

Deposit insurance provides a formal system for governments to deal with problems which may arise in the financial sector. This type of insurance also contributes to the restoration of confidence in the event of a failed financial institution. This protection also encourages savings. The Deposit Insurance Company was established in Trinidad and Tobago in 1986 following the failure of several financial institutions and has provided confidence and a cushion in the financial sector which has grown exponentially since 1986. Jamaica soon followed in 1998 and Barbados in 2006, joining countries like Germany, Canada, the USA, the UK, Venezuela, and India in setting up deposit insurance.

In Trinidad and Tobago depositors in all licensed financial institutions are insured up to a maximum of $125,000. Therefore, if an individual has $200,000 in a financial institution and that organization fails, the individual is only guaranteed to receive a maximum payment of $125,000.

Membership in the Fund is compulsory for all institutions licensed under the Financial Institution Act, 2008. Members of the Deposit Insurance Fund include commercial banks, finance houses and trust companies, and merchant banks. Here is a complete list of all the members of the Deposit Insurance Trust Fund:

- Commercial banks
  - Bank of Baroda (Trinidad and Tobago) Limited
  - Citibank (Trinidad and Tobago) Limited
  - First Caribbean International Bank (Trinidad and Tobago) Limited
  - First Citizens Bank Limited

  - Intercommercial Bank Limited
  - RBC Royal Bank (Trinidad & Tobago) Limited
  - Republic Bank Limited
  - Scotiabank Trinidad and Tobago Limited
- Finance houses
  - AIC Finance Limited
  - Caribbean Finance Company Limited
  - Fidelity Finance and Leasing Company Limited
  - General Finance Corporation Limited
  - Island Finance Trinidad and Tobago Limited.
- Trust companies and merchant banks
  - Ansa Merchant Bank Limited
  - Citicorp Merchant Bank Limited
  - Development Finance Limited
  - First Citizens Asset Management Limited
  - First Citizens Trustee Services Limited
  - Guardian Asset Management Limited
  - Intercommercial Trust and Merchant Bank Limited
  - RBC Investment Management (Caribbean) Limited
  - RBC Merchant Bank (Caribbean) Limited
  - RBC Trust (Trinidad & Tobago) Limited
  - Republic Finance and Merchant Bank Limited
  - Scotiatrust and Merchant Bank Trinidad and Tobago Limited.

The Deposit Insurance Company (DIC) was established by the Central Bank and Financial Institutions (Non-Banking) (Amendment) Act 1986, which provided for the creation of an ***independent fund from which depositors of failed financial institutions would be compensated or reimbursed.*** The Deposit Insurance Fund is financed mainly by initial contributions and annual premiums levied on licensed member-institutions and by matching initial contributions from the central bank. The DIC is empowered to borrow and special premiums may be levied on all member-institutions should the demand on the Fund exceed its resources. The introduction of the deposit insurance system has contributed to the building of confidence in financial institutions and the financial system as a whole.

Pursuant to Legal Notice No. 10 of 2012, the deposit insurance coverage limit has been increased from $75,000 to $125,000 per depositor in each capacity and right in each member-institution licensed under the Financial Institutions Act 2008. Deposit insurance continues to remain applicable only to those instruments that are covered under the Central Bank and Financial Institutions (Non-Banking) (Amendment) Act 1986 (Act No. 2 of 1986) namely, savings accounts, checking accounts, and time deposit accounts. Currently there are 25 member-institutions of the Deposit Insurance Fund.

Deposit insurance is of value and importance to all members of the public who hold deposits with licensed financial institution. All types of deposits received by a licensed institution in its usual course of business are insured. These include balances held on savings and checking accounts, demand deposits, and time deposits. The exceptions are letters of credit, stand-by letters credit and similar instruments, inter-bank deposits, deposits from affiliated companies, and foreign currency accounts. Certain cash liabilities, which an institution is primarily liable, such as cashier's checks, money orders, and drafts, are treated in the same manner as a deposit and added to any other deposits held in the same right and capacity by the claimant, and insured to a maximum of $125,000.

Deposit insurance is payable only when a licensed institution has been closed by the High Court as a result of action taken by the central bank. Foreign deposits are not covered by deposit insurance but only accounts held in Trinidad and Tobago dollars. Creditors other than depositors are also not covered by this type of insurance.

The insured limit is a maximum of $125,000 for each depositor in respect of deposits held in each insured institution in the following rights and capacities:

- Single (Individual) accounts
- Joint accounts
- Trust accounts (irrevocable express trust)

Making Claims

A depositor must file a claim for insurance on the official claim form within 12 months of the date of closure of the financial institution. Official claim forms are available from the DIC. It is advisable that claims be filed as soon as possible after the announcement of closure. Claims not filed within the 12-month period are not eligible for deposit insurance. If the 12-month period has passed, a creditor's claim by affidavit must then be filed with the Court-appointed Liquidator, which may be the DIC. The Liquidator is appointed when the Court makes a winding up order. Liquidation claims are required to be filed for all classes of creditors: preferential, secured, or unsecured. Those who are unable to attend in person may file claims by mail.

When more than one person is authorized to draw on the account, a claim must be filed by a person authorized to make withdrawals from the account. For example, a claim for deposit insurance on an account where either of two parties was authorized to sign for withdrawals may be made by either party. If two signatures were required to make withdrawals, both signatures will be required on the claim for deposit insurance.

To establish an insurance claim, every depositor will be required to provide original evidence of deposit ownership, such as a passbook, certificates of deposit, or other documents. Such documents must be made available for the claim to be processed in a timely manner.

Deposit Insurance Coverage

Deposit insurance provides coverage per institution. For instance, when a depositor has an account in the main office of an institution and also at a branch office, this is considered to be one institution. Therefore, the accounts will be added together and insured up to the $125,000 maximum. However, separately constituted subsidiaries or associated companies are recognized as distinct legal entities for deposit insurance purposes. Similarly, insurance protection is not increased by placing funds in two or more types of deposit accounts in the same institution. For example, checking and savings accounts held by the same depositor in the same right and capacity are added together and insured up to a maximum of $125,000.

When the DIC is informed that an institution has closed, it will balance the institution's books and credit interest earned on all accounts up to the date of closure. DIC officials will determine the net amount to be reimbursed to each depositor. A list of all deposits will be prepared. From this list, the following will be identified for further examination:

1. Depositors who have outstanding credit card balances or deposits pledged as collateral against their personal loans and/or overdrafts, and so on.
2. Depositors who have deposits pledged as collateral against loans taken by their friends and or relatives.
3. Depositors who have deposits pledged as collateral against their personal loans taken at another licensed member-institution.
4. Depositors who have funds in excess of the insured limit.

Thereafter, upon submission of a valid claim which is verified and approved, each eligible depositor will be paid up to a maximum of $125,000.

Financial transactions will be completed for the closed institution up to the closure date. Thus interest will only be paid on an account up to the date of closure, even if the maturity date of the account is beyond the date of closure. Likewise, checks which are not cleared on a depositor's account before the business of the institution is closed will not be paid or charged against the account. This is because of the action by the central bank to suspend the operations of the institution which will freeze all accounts at the date of suspension. Such checks will be returned and usually will be marked "drawee bank closed" or "refer to drawer." Therefore, this should not be reflected in the credit standing of the institution's depositor. However, it is the depositor's responsibility to make funds available to creditors who received checks that were returned and did not clear through the depositor's account because of the suspension of the institution.

If a depositor has a total claim of $130,000, he or she will be paid $125,000. Such depositor would then claim against the Liquidator of the closed institution for the remaining or excess which, in this case is $5000. In respect of this $5000, the depositor will be issued with a Liquidator's Certificate by the DIC. This certificate should then be presented to the Liquidator by the depositor who will be eligible to receive pro rata payment out of the assets of the institution, as and when they are realized or disposed of, in accordance with the laws of distribution in liquidation.

The DIC determines from the records of the institution how much a depositor should be paid, based on the principal balance on account with the institution, along with the interest accrued up to the date of the institution's closure. If this amount is not what the depositor expects to receive, the depositor must then provide proof to the DIC to substantiate his or her claim.

Joint Accounts

Individuals who hold joint and single accounts are treated a little differently. If each of the co-owners of the joint account has personally signed a valid account signature card and has right of withdrawal on the same basis as the other co-owners, the joint account and each of the individually owned accounts are separately insured up to the $125,000 maximum. (The execution of an account signature card is not required for time certificates of deposit or any other deposit obligations evidenced by a negotiable instrument, but the deposit must in law be jointly owned.) It should be noted that the insurance protection on joint accounts is not increased by rearranging the names of the owners, changing the style of the names, or by establishing more than one joint account for the same combination of owners in the same insured institution. No joint account shall in any case be entitled to insurance coverage in excess of $125,000.

All joint accounts owned by the same combination of individuals are first added together and the total is insured up to $125,000. In addition, the person's insurable interests in each joint account held by different combinations of individuals are added together and the total is insured up to the $125,000 maximum. Thus a person who has an interest in more than one joint account does not extend his or her insurance coverage. For example, assume that A and B own a joint account containing $140,000 and A and C own a joint account containing $80,000. The $140,000 account owned by A and B is insured up to $125,000, leaving $15,000 uninsured.

Since the interests of the co-owners of a joint account are deemed equal for insurance purposes (except in the case of a tenancy in common if unequal interests are shown on the account of the institution), the $125,000 is prorated equally between A and B, giving each an insurable interest of $62,500. The $80,000 in the other account is prorated equally between A and C, giving each a $40,000 insurable interest in that account. Thus, A has a total insurable interest of $102,500 (62,500 + 40,000) in the two accounts, and B and C have insurable interests of $62,500 and $40,000, respectively. Since no person's total insurable interest can exceed the $125,000 limit, the joint account of A and B will receive $125,000 in insurance whereas the joint account of A and C will receive $80,000.

Barbados

The Barbados Deposit Insurance Corporation (BDIC) is a statutory corporation which was established under the Deposit Insurance Act (2006). The BDIC commenced operations on June 8, 2007, and provides insurance coverage of up to BDS$25,000 for depositors of commercial banks, as well as deposit-taking trust and finance companies. The Barbados Deposit Insurance Corporation is an extension of the financial sector safety net, contributing to the maintenance of public confidence in deposit-taking institutions within the financial system.

Credit unions in Barbados in 2010 accepted the World Council of Credit Unions' (WOCCU) design for a program that will implement deposit insurance for the country's financial cooperatives which came on the heels of a signing ceremony held in Barcelona during the International Credit Union Conference in Barcelona, Spain, in 2009. The proposed program's implementation would not only strengthen the Caribbean nation's credit union movement but also enable it to compete more effectively with foreign banks that currently dominate the Barbados financial sector.

Credit unions are Barbados' only locally owned financial institutions and serve more than two-thirds of the population. However up to October 2017, the necessary amendments to the relevant pieces of legislation to give credit union members the same level of protection as that enjoyed by the customers of commercial banks and finance companies were not passed.

Jamaica

Under the Deposit Insurance Act of 1998, the Jamaica Deposit Insurance Corporation (JDIC) is vested with the responsibility to manage the scheme governed by this Act and is a safety net set up primarily to protect depositors in case their bank or other insured financial institution fails or is unable to make payments on deposits. Deposit insurance also covers credit unions.

Exercise

A and B have a joint account containing $120,000, A and C have a joint account containing $109,000, A and D an account containing $106,000, and A and E an account containing $65,000, the aggregate of A's prorated interest in the four accounts amounts to $200,000. However, A's interest in each joint account will be reduced by $75,000 or 3/8th (Excess of Coverage Limit/Aggregated Prorated Interest = $75,000/ $200,000) so as to restrict total insurance payable to A to $125,000. Therefore, the value of A's interest in each account will be calculated at 5/8th of the amount in the account.

The interest of a beneficiary in a valid irrevocable express trust is insured up to $125,000, separately from the individual accounts of the settlor, the trustees, or other beneficiaries. However, all trust interests created by the same settlor (grantor) in the same institution for the same beneficiary will be added together and insured in the aggregate up to a maximum of $125,000.

Payment of Insured Deposits

When an institution has been closed by the central bank and a winding up order is issued by the Court, each depositor will be notified in writing at the depositor's last address on record with the institution. This notification will be mailed shortly after the institution closes. Notification will also be given in the press. The DIC is statutorily obligated to commence payment to depositors within three(3) months of closure of an institution. Information regarding the date and place of payment will be posted on the doors of the closed institution, published in the press, and indicated in notices sent to depositors. Those depositors whose accounts are subject to further examination will be requested to meet with the relevant DIC officials. When the DIC has instructions to effect payment to depositors, it will do so by means of checks up to the insured limit to be collected at the DIC's office or other location as indicated by the DIC.

Deposit Transfer

The DIC transfers an amount equivalent to the total insured deposits of an institution, under an agreement which will enable depositors of the failed institution to collect their entitlements from a financial institution serving as the Paying Agent. The DIC will notify depositors of the transfer of deposits and of the place and time that the deposits can be withdrawn from the financial institution serving as the Paying Agent. The depositor has to satisfy the DIC or the Paying Agent that he/she is the rightful owner of the deposit claimed. In cases of doubt, the Paying Agent may refer the matter to the DIC. A depositor, if he/she wishes, can open an account, in cases where the Paying Agent is a viable financial institution, for the full amount or part of his/her deposit.

Depositors with Loan Accounts

When a financial institution is closed, any outstanding loans that the depositor has in the institution must still be paid. When acting as Liquidator of a closed institution, the DIC is acting on behalf of all creditors of that institution and its obligation is to collect all loans promptly and efficiently along with other assets of the institution. The Corporation can offset the balance on a deposit account, including any uninsured portion, against a loan if the loan and deposit are held by the same person or persons.

Recovery of Uninsured Balances

The DIC will issue certificates (Liquidator Certificates) to cover the value of deposits in excess of the insured maximum of $125,000 as well as other uninsured claims against the failed institution. Payments, called dividends, depend on the rate of recovery from the liquidation of assets of the institution, and the extent and priority of claims from other creditors of the institution. Initial and final disbursements may take up to several years, depending on but not limited to, the pace of realization of the assets, the overall state of the macro-economy, and so on. Shareholders of a failed institution recover their investment only after all depositors and other creditors receive payments in full on their claims, including interest, in accordance with the laws governing liquidation.

Life Insurance

Life insurance is a contract between the insurance policy holder and an insurance company whereby the insurer pays the beneficiary of the insured person an agreed sum as determined by the premium and terms of the policy. On death of the insured the sum received under a life insurance policy will help with funeral expenses, clear off outstanding debt, such as mortgage.

Whole life insurance covers the individual for his/her entire life once all the premiums are paid. Premiums are fixed for the duration of the policy and are determined by the age of the individual at first issuance and the amount of coverage requested. Whole life insurance belongs to the cash value category of life insurance.

Term life insurance offers coverage for a fixed premium for a fixed duration of time. Thus if the person dies within the term, his or her beneficiary will be paid the death benefit. If he or she survives the specified term no benefit will be due or payable to the insured. Term life insurance is the cheapest option to purchase and is used with mortgages as it offers additional security to the mortgagee.

An endowment life policy is designed to pay a lump sum payment at maturity or death. The maturity date can be set to 10, 15, or 20 years in the future and up to an age limit. Some policies also pay the lump sum for critical illness. This type of policy can be cashed in early and the policy holder will receive the surrender value.

An investment-linked plan offers life insurance and investment within one plan. Thus with this type of policy there is an opportunity to make gains on your contributions. Some plans also allow the opportunity to invest more by allowing payments larger than premium. The gains you make will be dependent on how well the insurance company invests your money and the general performance of the financial market.

There are various types of insurance namely. A helpful hint is the younger you are when you take out life insurance, the lower the premium which can give you the ability to take out a larger coverage.

Motor Vehicle Insurance

Motor vehicle insurance protects third parties and in the case of full comprehensive insurance, the car owner against financial loss due to unpredictable events like automobile accidents, fires, and natural disasters. The insurance company in which the policy was established will make payments directly to third parties for injury or damage to property caused by the insured vehicle in an accident. The minimum third-party insurance is mandatory by law in Trinidad and Tobago for any vehicle being driven in a public place. The Motor Vehicle Insurance (Third Party Risks) Act, Chap 48:51, requires that, at a minimum, every motor vehicle must be insured against third-party risks. It is therefore compulsory for all vehicles to carry at least third-party motor insurance cover for use on all public roads.

General insurance companies offer motor insurance policies to meet different needs that consumers may have. There are three main types of vehicle insurance: fully comprehensive, third party only, and third party fire and theft.

Fully comprehensive policies provide the widest coverage. The policy protects the owner from financial loss for damage to insured vehicle caused by accidents, fire, and theft. A private comprehensive insurance can provide additional benefits without any additional premium. Some of these benefits include damage to garage by fire, medical expenses incurred in respect of occupants in the vehicle following the accident, personal accident coverage to insured/spouse, and clothing and personal effects. However, coverage against losses caused by natural perils such as flood, hurricanes, or earthquakes, as well as cover for breakage of windscreens can be purchased at an additional cost.

Comprehensive Motor Insurance

Comprehensive motor insurance is a requirement to protect the mortgagee's interest in the vehicle in the event the vehicle is destroyed or stolen for vehicles that are subject to a mortgage bill of sale. While this is the most desirable cover, it is the costliest and insurers also have restrictions on granting comprehensive cover based on the age, condition, and type of the vehicle. It is important that the insured gives full and complete disclosure to the insurance agent to ensure validity of insurance policy and recovery if claim is subsequently made for losses incurred. The agent will ascertain whether the vehicle can be covered under a comprehensive motor policy.

Comprehensive insurance covers physical loss or damage to your motor vehicle caused by:

- accidental collision and overturning,
- fire or lightning explosion,
- Burglary, housebreaking, or theft, and
- Riot, civil commotion, strike, and malicious damage.

Comprehensive insurance covers your own damage and liability to third parties. Coverage of liability to third parties is required by law. The features and benefits offered under a comprehensive policy vary from one company to another and ***it is important that you understand what is or is not covered by the particular policy***. If you are not sure, ask your broker, insurer, or its agent for specific details when you are purchasing your policy contract. Some insurers extend their comprehensive policy to include hurricane, earthquake, and flood in their standard coverage while others provide this cover for an additional premium.

Third Party Insurance

Third party insurance policy does not provide financial compensation to the insured in the event of an accident but rather only to the third party for damage incurred as a result of the insured vehicle/driver. It is the minimum mandatory insurance cover required by the Motor Vehicle Act in Trinidad and Tobago for a vehicle being driven in a public area. The cost for this cover is therefore lower than comprehensive or fire and theft policies.

A third party motor vehicle policy will only respond to pay to third parties for injury or damage to property caused by the insured in an accident. The insured under a private motor vehicle policy may also obtain the following benefits for additional premiums:

- Flood, hurricane, earthquake, volcanic eruption, riot, and strike, and
- Windscreen breakage claims as an additional benefit or extension not subject to any excess and without affecting the insured's safe driver discount

Currently, the minimum third party insurance cover limits are as follows:

- Third-party death or bodily injury: Sum of $1 million for any one claim by any one person and limited to $2 million, in respect of all claims, arising out of any one accident
- Third-party property damage: Sum of $500,000 for any one claim by any one person and limited to $1 million, in respect of all claims arising out of any one accident.

Full Third Party Plus Fire and Theft

A full third party fire and theft policy provides wider coverage than a third party policy. In addition to third party liability, coverage is extended to the risk of fire and theft of your motor vehicle. However, this policy does not cover collision damage to your own vehicle as is the case of comprehensive insurance. Underwriting standards vary among insurance companies. For example, some companies will not offer comprehensive cover for motor vehicles that are considered old, that is, more than five years old. Instead, they would offer insurance cover against third party fire and theft risks only for such motor vehicles.

Third-party fire and theft would protect the owner from financial loss for damage to the vehicle caused by fire or theft only. The policy will also respond to pay third parties for injury or damage to property caused by you in an accident.

Sum Insured

A motor vehicle owner should ensure that the sum insured under the insurance policy represents the current market value of the vehicle. Market value is defined as the amount of money a buyer is prepared to pay and the seller is willing to accept in the open market. The market value is determined by the age of the motor vehicle, its condition, the accumulated mileage, and the demand for that type of motor vehicle in the used car market. Two motor vehicles of the same age can therefore fetch vastly different prices. Insurance companies use pre-determined depreciation rates to calculate each year the suggested sum insured of a motor vehicle. However, they would usually advise you (the insured) to obtain an independent valuation of your vehicle, particularly if you are not in agreement with the sum insured as calculated by the company.

Limitations to Use

If a motor vehicle is licensed for private use, **that is,** ***carrying "P" registration plates, it should not be used for hire, that is, to be rented or***

used as "ph" (private hire). Registered taxis carry "H" registration plates while rented motor vehicles are usually recognized by registration plates beginning with "R." The insurance company will not honor any claims arising from any accident when the motor vehicle is being operated contrary to the use for which it is insured.

One example is the use of private cars for hire by their owners. In many areas in Trinidad and Tobago, it is quite common for commuters to travel in private cars or "ph" taxis as they are commonly known. ***Passengers should bear in mind that in the event of injury as a result of an accident, while in a "ph" taxi, they will not be entitled to any compensation from the insurance company. The owner of the motor vehicle should also be aware that he or she will be personally liable for any property damage*** (e.g., third party's vehicle, fence, house, etc.) arising out of an accident in which the motor vehicle is involved.

Young and Inexperienced Drivers

The insurance industry defines young drivers as persons under the age of 25 years and inexperienced drivers as persons who have had a valid driver's permit for less than two years or those who have not been driving regularly, even though they may have had their permit for more than two years.

Open Versus Restricted Coverage

Most insurance companies no longer issue open policies where anyone, who with the owner's consent, is permitted to drive the vehicle, including young and inexperienced drivers. Most standard insurance policies require that anyone who is permitted to drive the vehicle must be over the age of 25 years and have at least two years' driving experience. Some companies restrict the use of the vehicle to drivers named on the insurance certificate only, for example, the insured and his/her spouse. Cover may be extended to young and/or inexperienced drivers upon the payment of an additional premium.

Policy Excess or Deductible

Comprehensive

A policy excess or deductible is a common feature of a comprehensive insurance policy and it represents the portion of each claim that the insured must absorb. This measure elimiminates small and minor "nuisance" claims. The policy excess is usually calculated as a percentage of the sum insured and may be set at a minimum amount. For example, if the percentage of the sum insured is calculated to be $15,000 but the minimum excess is $2000, then the insurance company will deduct the minimum excess of $2000 from any claim settlement.

The amount of policy excess that is applied can vary from one insurer to another and depends on the type of loss suffered. For example,

- Own damage (physical damage to your own vehicle),
- Fire and/or lightning,
- Theft, depending on whether or not an anti-theft device was installed, and
- Breakage of glass.

A higher policy excess is normally applied in respect of any young drivers permitted to drive under the policy.

According to the terms of the policy contract, some insurance companies might impose an excess on a third party policy, for example, $1000 for third party property damage claims, for example, another motor vehicle, fence, and so on. ***The excess is an arrangement under the contract, where the policyholder must be prepared to repay the insurer when a third party claim is settled, usually in exchange for a lower premium.*** The law requires the insurance company to settle a claim when its client is liable notwithstanding that there is an arrangement between the insurer and the insured. This excess is not applicable to a third party who has presented a claim. An insurance company that imposes an excess on its insured cannot refuse to honor a claim from an innocent third party on the grounds that its policyholder has not paid his or her excess to the insurance company.

No Claim Discount

A No Claim Discount (NCD) is an insurance company's way of rewarding policyholders for being "claims free." On the other hand, where the claims experience is not good, there may be a loss of the NCD or even the application of a loading or increase to the premium at the next renewal date of the policy. NCD is earned on each insured vehicle. However, it can be transferred to a second vehicle in order to reduce the premium that may be charged on that vehicle. A NCD is tied to the owner of the vehicle and he or she retains the benfit even when the current vehicle is sold as the NCD is transferred to any vehicle the owner subsequently owns.

The maximum limits on NCDs may vary from one insurer to another. On a comprehensive policy, the limit may range between 25% and 65% of the premium. In the case of a third party policy, the limit varies between 20% and 40% of the premium.

There is generally a misunderstanding regarding the loss of an NCD when a claim is presented by a policyholder who was not liable for the accident or event. Under a comprehensive policy, your insurer will settle your own damage claim and have your vehicle repaired. Your insurer will then seek to recover the amount paid out from the liable party's insurer. Until this amount is recovered, your insurance company is entitled to withhold your NCD in accordance with the policy conditions. If the amount paid out is received in full, the NCD will be reinstated. If not, it may be prorated as indicated above.

In the event of a claim, insurers do not usually take away the full NCD but may reduce it. Some insurance companies have introduced the concept of protecting your NCD in certain circumstances. For example, if you have the benefit of 60% NCD and you have a claim, your NCD might be reduced to between 50% and 40%, depending on the claim amount and not reduced to zero after the first claim. However, after two or three consecutive claims within a short period of time, the NCD may be taken away fully or, your insurance company may decide to cancel your insurance policy because of the frequency of claims.

Subrogation: This is a legal concept that allows one insurer who has settled the cost of a claim to eventually recover those payments from the person legally liable (usually from the insurer of the liable party). Normally this is done by sending a notice of subrogation to the insurer of the party at fault. The amount the insurer is seeking to recover will often include the policy excess and other uninsured losses, for example, loss of use.

When your insurance company recovers the amount paid out, it will reimburse you for the policy excess that you may have paid or that was deducted from the settlement previously paid to you. However, your policy may also allow for a pro rata refund of your excess if your company does not collect 100% of the amount demanded. Your responsibility in the subrogation process is to give your insurer full and complete cooperation. It means that you should not interfere with your insurance company's attempt to recover payments made on your behalf.

Liability to Third Parties

The law does not permit an insurance company to deny liability to a third party even if the driver of the insured motor vehicle was not operating in accordance with the terms of the insurance contract. The insurance company can refuse to pay its client's own damage, that is, the damage to your own motor vehicle under the full comprehensive section of the policy, since you are in breach of your contract. However, it cannot deny a third party property or personal injury claim if liability has been established. Normally, an insurance company will settle these third party claims but it is entitled to recover its payout from you personally.

Driving Without Insurance

You will be considered to be "driving without insurance" if you cannot produce a valid certificate of insurance as required under the Motor Vehicle Insurance (Third Party Risks) Act when asked to do so by an authorized officer (i.e., policeman or licensing officer) when driving your motor vehicle.

Transfer of Unexpired Insurance Coverage

Some motor vehicle owners sell their vehicles with the unexpired insurance as part of the deal. This is against the law. Insurance cover cannot be transferred from one insured to another. Each insured must complete a proposal form with his or her insurer and the premium is determined based on the information submitted. When a motor vehicle is sold, the vendor must surrender the certificate of insurance to his insurer. If he or she so wishes, arrangements can be made to have the unexpired portion of the premium credited to the purchaser who must effect his own insurance cover separately.

Claim Against Registered Owner

In the event of a claim arising out of an accident caused by an uninsured vehicle, the only recourse is for the injured party to take action against the registered owner of the motor vehicle through the courts. Please understand that there are risks with taking action as this can be costly, time-consuming, and may not produce the desired results unless the registered owner has the means to pay any awards that may be made by the courts. ***It is very important that you ensure that upon sale (or other form of disposal) of your motor vehicle, ownership is legally transferred at the Licensing Office of the Transport Division as required by law. By doing so, you will avoid any unwanted liability.***

Purchasing Motor Vehicle Insurance

When purchasing motor insurance, one is required to present the following documents to your broker, the insurance company, or its agent:

- Certified copy of ownership of vehicle,
- Valid driver's permit (including that of intended driver/s),
- Passport or National Identification Card,
- No Claim Discount letter from your previous insurer (where applicable), and
- Pro forma invoice (for new vehicle/s).

One is also required to complete a motor insurance proposal form. It is critically important that questions are answered truthfully and correctly and to the best of one's knowledge. It is good practice to report any previous claims and accidents, even if claims were not made to the insurance company.

Helpful Hints

The law and good practice requires that the insurance company be provided with the relevant information if the insured vehicle is modified or changed, including any variations in the cc rating that can increase the vehicle's speed, any change in color, or any additional accessories such as mag rims and tires for updating of records. Persons not included in the proposal form should not be allowed to drive the vehicle as this is a breach of the terms and invalidates the insurance cover. If the facts are misrepresented on the proposal form to obtain a more favorable premium, this may be considered a breach of the policy contract. For example, if the contract states that the vehicle is kept in a locked garage but it is actually parked on the roadside at night and it is stolen, the insurer will not pay your claim. It is important that owing to the portability (on wheels) vehicles should be properly secured at all times, kept in a locked garage if possible. Discounts are additional benfits that are also granted where motor vehicles are equipped with anti-theft devices and/or completing a defensive driving course. However, the insurance company can deny a claim if a vehicle is stolen and it is discovered that the anti-theft device was not activated at the time the vehicle was stolen. Before renewing an insurance policy, it is recommended that a current valuation and condition survey be done and submitted to the insurance company to ensure that the sum insured is adequate and within the market value range as this will be used for settlement of the claim rather than an arbitrary settlement amount.

Certificate of Insurance

The Motor Vehicle Insurance (Third Party Risks) Act, Chap 48:51, Section 5 requires that a certificate of insurance be issued as evidence that there is an insurance policy in force that covers personal injury and property damage caused by the motor vehicle. Motorists are required to produce a valid certificate of insurance on demand by a law enforcement officer or an officer of the Transport and Licensing Authority.

The insurer is required by law to prepare the relevant motor insurance policy document within seven days of receipt of the premium from the insured. However, an insurance certificate is normally given to the insured at the time of purchase and the insured is required to keep it in a safe place, either on his or her person or in the motor vehicle. Section 14 of the Motor Vehicle Insurance Act requires that an insured driver return the certificate of insurance when the insurance policy is canceled by the insurer, either by mutual consent or because of a provision in the policy. If this is not returned, the law requires the insurance company to institute legal action against the insured for the return of the certificate of insurance. Otherwise, the insurance company can be held responsible for liability to a third party as the insurance would be deemed to be valid.

Genuine Brokers and Agents

It is important that the selected broker or agent is registered. If in doubt, ask them to show you their current certificate of registration from the Central Bank of Trinidad and Tobago and verify the information. Some insurers extend the provisions of their motor insurance policy to include roadside assistance as a benefit. The insurance company generally contracts with a third party to provide such services. Normally this will include:

- Free towing in instances of a mechanical breakdown or after an accident,
- Flat tire assistance,
- Breakdown due to battery problems or lack of fuel, and
- Lock service (should you lock your keys in the vehicle).

This benefit can be included for an additional charge to your premium. However, the use of this service will not affect your "No Claim Discount."

How to Make a Claim: Motor Vehicle Accident

In the case of a major accident:

1. Call the police immediately.
2. Mark the position of the vehicles at the point of impact.
3. If possible, remove your vehicle to the side of the road to allow for the free passage of traffic provided there is/are no serious personal injury or fatalities.

   (In the case of a minor accident)
4. Exchange the following information with the other party involved:

   - Driving permit number
   - Insurance certificate of the vehicle.

   Take down the following information from the certificate(s) of insurance:

   - Insurance company of other party
   - Policy/certificate number(s)
   - Name(s) of owner(s) of the vehicle(s)
   - Period of insurance (and expiry date)
   - Any other information in respect of the names of persons permitted to drive.

5. If possible, obtain the names, addresses, and telephone contact numbers of any witnesses in any other vehicle/vehicles and any other independent witnesses to the accident.
6. ***DO NOT ACCEPT LIABILITY.*** It is a condition of your policy that you do not accept liability for the accident. You should therefore comply with the terms of the insurance policy.
7. Secure your vehicle and do not leave it unattended. Call for a tow vehicle if your vehicle cannot be driven and have it taken to a garage, safe place, or your home.
8. Report the accident to the nearest police station and ensure that it is properly recorded in the station diary. Provide a full account of the accident and the names of witnesses and ensure that the police officer

has taken the information accurately. Read the statement for accuracy. Take note of the police officer's name and badge number.

9. Failure to report an accident is an offense (Section 79 of the Motor Vehicle and Road Traffic Act, Chap. 48:50). If the accident is considered to be minor, there may be a verbal agreement between the parties involved not to report the matter to the police. However, there may be a change of heart by the other party/parties involved and this may leave you open to prosecution. The best advice is for you to report the accident to the police, however minor it may appear at the time.

If you are making a claim, you must do the following:

1. Complete the motor vehicle accident claim form with your insurer.
2. Submit the following to the insurance company:
   - Estimate for repairs (clearly itemized),
   - Information on the third party's vehicle such as the registration number, owner's name, and the name of the driver,
   - Statement or letter from your insurer if you are claiming from third party insurer,
   - Proof of ownership (certified copy of motor vehicle registration),
   - Original receipts for doctor's or hospital fees (in the case of a claim for personal or passenger injuries),
   - Pictures of your damaged car (if available),
   - Proof of identification,
   - Letter from the VAT office advising your VAT status, and
   - An up-to-date inspection certificate, where necessary.

When settling a claim, the insurer will apply the principle of indemnity, that is, the final settlement the insured receives places him in a similar position that he would be in prior to the accident. Disagreements tend to arise between the claimant and the insurer regarding the application of this principle. In many instances claimants suffer financially as replacement cost of parts is usually more than the amount received from the insurance company. The insurer will usually adjust the estimated figures downward owing mainly to the concept of depreciation of the asset. The claimant is not expected to be in a better position as a result of his or her misfortune. Unfortunately albeit an asset may be insured for many years, the replacement cost of a damaged part would cost the same as for a new vehicle but the settlement is normally adjusted for the age of the asset.

A motor vehicle is a depreciating asset and its value decreases over time. The reduction in value begins as soon as the new vehicle leaves the car showroom. The market value of a vehicle is determined by a number of factors such as the type of vehicle, its use and maintenance, accumulated mileage, and physical condition of the vehicle. Market value and not the sum insured is the basis of the valuation of the vehicle at the time of loss and this is determined by a registered loss adjuster. The assessment will be based on the current market value, which is usually lower than the sum insured owing to depreciation of the asset.

When the replacement parts are "foreign used" parts, there is usually no contribution toward the cost of the part required by the claimant. When "foreign used or used" parts are not available, the insurer will allow a new part to be used as a replacement. However, the claimant will be required to contribute toward the cost of this new part since this new replacement part is "betterment" as the vehicle is no longer new.

Procedure for Making a Motor Vehicle Insurance Claim for Physical Damages

- Provide the insurance company with a full and accurate account of the accident on the claim form and take care to include all the relevant facts.
- It is normal for an insurer to conduct investigations into the circumstances surrounding an accident in which one of their insured vehicles is involved. You should therefore cooperate with the investigator if one is appointed.
- Note that an adjuster may be appointed to survey the damage to your vehicle. He will determine whether the labor cost is adequate and whether the damaged parts can be repaired or should be replaced. Generally, his report to the insurance company will guide the final settlement that is made for your claim.
- Ensure that you pay any applicable excess in order to expedite repairs to your vehicle in the case of a claim under a comprehensive policy.

Procedure for making a claim for Theft of Motor Vehicle

In the event of theft of a motor vehicle, you should take the following actions:

1. Report the disappearance of the vehicle immediately to the nearest police station.
2. Notify your insurance company and complete the necessary claim form.
3. Cooperate with the insurance investigator. It is the normal practice for the insurance company to engage the services of an investigator to verify the circumstances surrounding the claim.
3. Pay any applicable policy excess as stated in your policy.
4. Deliver the set of spare keys to the insurer.
5. Sign the motor vehicle transfer form. In the event that the vehicle is recovered after the claim is settled, the insurer will have title to the vehicle.
6. Produce a letter from the VAT Office advising of your VAT status.

Helpful Hint

Most insurers wait approximately six weeks before settling a claim for theft. This gives sufficient time for a full investigation to be conducted by the investigator and the police. It also provides adequate time for the vehicle to be recovered.

Personal Injury

Persons who suffer injury in a motor vehicle accident are entitled to compensation from the person who is at fault in the accident. The insurer for the driver of the motor vehicle that is liable in the accident will be required to pay compensation (damages). ***An injured party has four years (limited by law) within which to make a claim for personal injury; thereafter any right to file a suit against the insurance company will be lost.***

In the event of a personal injury claim, you will be required to submit the following information:

1. Full medical report on injury and treatment received for the injury sustained in the accident.
2. Bills and receipts for expenses incurred.
3. Estimated costs of any further treatment or corrective surgery required as a result of your injury as confirmed by a doctor.
4. Details of any loss of wages or earnings.
5. An assessment of disability and the impact on your ability to work in the future.

Helpful Hint

A claim for personal injury is often complicated and may require that you obtain legal advice during the process.

Claim in Excess of the Amount Insured

The law does not release the owner of a motor vehicle from liability in the event that there is a court award that is higher than the insured limit in the policy. For example, if the claim for personal injury is $3 million, the insurer may settle the third party to the limit of $2 million as required by law. Assuming that the insurer did not issue a policy for a higher limit, the claimant can still seek to recover the balance of $1 million from the liable party (the owner of the vehicle). Vehicle owners must therefore pay attention to the limits of liability stated in their policy.

Writs or Summons

After an accident, the owner of the vehicle involved in the accident or third parties (e.g., passengers or pedestrians) may file a writ against the person who, in their opinion, is responsible for the accident resulting in damage. ***Upon receipt of a writ or summons from a court or a letter***

threatening the filing of any action by an attorney-at-law, you are required to immediately contact your insurance company. There is a time frame of eight days within which the insured must enter an appearance in court in his or her defense, failing which the plaintiff can obtain judgment by default.

Complaints Process at the Office of the Financial Services Ombudsman (OFSO)

The Office of the Financial Services Ombudsman (OFSO) provides an avenue for resolving complaints against an insurance company to mitigate against claims reaching the courts. The services provided are free and are available to individuals and small companies whose assets (excluding real estate) do not exceed $1.5 million. Where a dispute arises and cannot be amicably resolved between a consumer and an insurance company, the consumer can approach the OFSO for assistance if the complaint meets the following criteria:

- *Undue Delay*
    - More than 60 days have elapsed since lodging the claim at the insurance company and no final decision has been reached.
- *Denial of Liability*
    - The insurance company has denied liability for the consumer's claim and the consumer has reasonable evidence to support otherwise.
- *Inadequate offer*
    - The insurance company has offered to settle the consumer's claim, but the consumer believes that the amount being offered is inadequate to cover his losses.

If a complaint falls in one of the above categories, the consumer must complete the prescribed complaint form and submit it along with copies of all supporting documents. The OFSO has the authority to mediate in the following instances:

- Where the amount in dispute in any type of insurance is less than $500,000
- In the case of a motor vehicle accident, where the claim for physical damage to property caused to a third party is not more than $25,000

The OFSO, however, does not handle complaints relating to third party personal injury claims.

The OFSO uses mediation to settle the disputes between the insurer and the complainant where necessary. In accordance with the mediation process, the complainant has the option to withdraw at any time and refer the dispute to another forum. Mediation process is not binding on either party and where the parties cannot reach a mutually acceptable solution, the Financial Services Ombudsman can make a recommendation for settlement and/or finalize an award on behalf of the complainant up to a limit of $500,000. Once accepted by the complainant, an award is binding on the insurance company and must not be greater than the amount required to compensate the complainant for direct loss or damage suffered. When the award is paid in full and final settlement is made the matter is then considered resolved. The complainant cannot approach the insurance company at any time in the future on any issue relating to the same claim.

Glossary of Terms

- *Accident*
    - An unforeseen event that usually results in a loss
- *Adjuster*

- Same as a loss adjuster, he or she is a person appointed by an insurer or insured to assess and quantify the extent of damages to claims; adjusters are licensed by the Central Bank.

- *Agent*

  - Person who acts on behalf of an insurance company and usually accepts proposals for insurance for a commission; agents are licensed by the Central Bank.

- *Casualty Liability*

  - A loss arising out of an accident

- *Casualty Insurance*

  - Class of insurance business that covers liability or financial loss arising out of an accident and payments of compensation to third parties who suffer bodily injury or death

- *Claim*

  - A demand for payment of compensation or other benefits under a policy of insurance

- *Commissions*

  - Amount/monies paid by an insurer to an agent or broker for placing policies

- *Contribution*

  - Refers to the way two or more insurance policies covering the same risk will share the loss; however, locally it commonly refers to the amount an insured will pay toward the cost of a new replacement part in motor claims when a used part is not available.

- *Contributory Negligence*
  - The sharing of liability by the claimants involved in an accident
- *Constructive Total Loss*
  - An insurer will declare an asset to be a CTL if it is deemed uneconomical to repair—usually when the repair cost is 50% or more of the actual market value of the asset.
- *Complaint*
  - A grievance or dissatisfaction about a service or compensation being offered; individuals with complaints against insurance companies can take them to the Office of the Financial Services Ombudsman at the Central Bank of Trinidad and Tobago, Independence Square, Port of Spain.
- *Comprehensive Insurance*
  - Comprehensive insurance in the local context includes a wide range of cover but is nonetheless subject to exclusions and conditions and not all policies provide identical cover, so it is advisable to review the policy contract.
- *Deductible*
  - An amount that the insured must bear before the insurer pays, also referred to as a policy excess; if the claim is below the deductible, no amount is payable by the insurer.
- *Depreciation*
  - The decrease in the value of an asset over time as most assets have a limited useful life; at the time of a loss, the value is established by applying a depreciation factor to reflect the remaining useful life of the asset.

- *Discharge Form*
    - A form which a claimant is required to sign on settlement of a claim, which states that the insurer's liability has been fully settled and no further claim arising out of the same event can be presented.
- *Excess*
    - Same as deductible; an amount that the insured must bear before the insurer pays. If the claim is below the excess, no amount is payable by the insurer.
- *Exclusions*
    - Terms in an insurance policy under which the insurer will not pay if loss sustained is caused by an event or peril that is not covered.
- *Exposure*
    - The measurement of risk.
- *Office of The Financial Services Ombudsman (OFSO)*
    - The complaints authority established and funded by commercial banks and insurance companies which individuals and small businesses with complaints can approach for resolution at no cost to the complainants; final decisions of the Ombudsman are binding on the insurer but the complainant is free to seek other legal remedies if not satisfied with the decision of the OFSO.
- *Fraudulent misrepresentation*
    - The deliberate provision of wrong and/or misleading information to an insurer when making an application for insurance; an insurer can deny a claim if the information provided is material and fraudulent.

- *Indemnity*

  - A key insurance principle which states that the policyholder should be returned to the same position that he/she was in immediately prior to the loss; there must be neither gain nor loss. Insurance is not meant for a policyholder to profit from a loss.

- *Insurance Broker*

  - Is an independent licensed insurance adviser who acts on behalf of his client when placing insurance cover with an insurer; he usually receives commissions from the insurer. In some instances he may earn fees from his client; unlike an agent, he may obtain quotations from different insurers. Brokers are licensed by the Central Bank.

- *Liability*

  - An obligation on a policyholder to pay damages arising out of an event; the obligation can be legally enforced.

- *Loss of Use*

  - This is considered an uninsured loss. In the event of a motor claim, the insurance company will compensate the claimant for "Loss of Use" using a per-day monetary value. Payment is calculated by multiplying the daily rate by the number of days that the adjuster estimates it will take to repair the vehicle.

- *Market Value*

  - The current price of an asset (a motor vehicle) that a buyer will pay and a seller will accept.

- *Material Fact*
    - Information that, if disclosed, will influence the decision of a prudent underwriter and therefore must be made known to the insurance company at the time of providing information.
- *Misrepresentation*
    - Misrepresentation can be innocent or fraudulent. Innocent misrepresentation is unlikely to affect insurance cover after the passage of time. On the other hand, fraudulent misrepresentation is "fraud" since it is deemed to be deliberate and intended to mislead the insurer and can render the policy void and of no effect. No claim may therefore be paid.
- *No Claim Discount (NCD)*
    - This is a system of reward to a motor vehicle owner if he/she has a "claims-free" record. Each year a discount is earned until the maximum limit is reached.
- *Occurrence*
    - An event (a loss) which triggers payment
- *Renewal*
    - The offer by an insurer to a policyholder to insure the risk for another period, usually a further period of one year at the expiration of the policy
- *Risk*
    - Often referred to as the probability of a loss: financial, physical, or otherwise.

- *Salvage*
  - The value of an asset (motor vehicle) in its damaged condition or the disposable value of the wreck which can be sold for its parts
- *Subrogation*
  - The right of the insurer, after settling a claim, to pursue recovery against the party that is responsible for the loss, usually against the insurer of the liable party
- *Sum Insured*
  - The amount stated in the policy; it represents the limit that the insurer will pay in the event of a total loss.
- *Term*
  - Insured period
- *Third Party*
  - The person who may have been injured or whose property was damaged, other than the insured or the insurer
- *Total Loss*
  - The complete destruction of insured property where there is no salvage or residual value
- *Underwriter*
  - A person in an insurance company who assesses risks and is authorized to accept or refuse cover at a given premium and under given terms and conditions

- *Utmost Good Faith*

    - A key insurance principle which states that all parties must act on the basis of trust; however, the applicant for insurance has a duty to provide all information that will assist the underwriter in assessing the risk in order to arrive at an appropriate premium. Generally, in the commercial sector, the principle is known as, "let the buyer beware."

- *Valuation*

    - A value placed on property for insurance purposes; for example, a motor vehicle has to be valued in order to determine the sum at which it should be insured.

What Do I Need in Order to Get Motor Vehicle Insurance?

You need the following documents in order to get motor vehicle insurance:

- Completed proposal form
- Two forms of photo identification
- A recent utility bill
- Certified copy of ownership, or pro forma invoice for vehicle to be insured
- Proof of all discounts
- Government inspection certificate for vehicles five years and older from date of manufacture

Home or Property Insurance

For most persons their home may be their largest investment. It is therefore imperative that home insurance is secured to protect the investment from loss by fire or other disasters. The purpose of home or property insurance is to assist the homeowner in restoring his home and/or property if damaged by natural disasters or other perils. Home insurance, also commonly called hazard insurance or homeowner's insurance is a type of property insurance that covers a private residence. This policy can be combined with various personal insurance protections, which can include losses occurring to one's home, its contents, loss of use (additional living expenses), or loss of other personal possessions of the homeowner, as well as liability insurance for accidents that may happen at home or at the hands of the homeowner within the policy territory.

Property insurance is a policy that provides financial reimbursement to the owner or renter of a structure and its contents in the event of damage or theft. Property insurance can include homeowner's insurance, renter's insurance, flood insurance, and earthquake insurance. Property insurance is available to cover risks to property posed due to threats and perils such as fire, theft, and weather damage. This is a comprehensive policy; it can be further made available into more specific and specialized forms such as fire insurance, flood insurance, earthquake, home, and boiler insurance. Home insurance on the other hand offers cover for structural damages caused to the house due to natural calamities or man-made threats. While property insurance is available for home or other kinds of real estate, home insurance is restricted to homes.

Master Policy

It is common practice in Trinidad and Tobago for mortgagees and lenders and in particular, mortgage companies, to have an arrangement whereby all borrowers in a given development, in particular for townhouses and apartments, must obtain insurance coverage under a master policy either with one insurer or a group of insurers. The purpose of this is twofold:

- It allows for easy administration by mortgage companies since they do not have to track different expiry dates of insurance coverage for each of their borrowers, as the master policy has a common expiry date for all members.
- It allows for some negotiation of competitive premiums since each borrower receives only a certificate of insurance rather than a policy

document, resulting in a reduction of the insurance company's costs. The lender can also earn a volume discount as all borrowers are covered under a single contract.

The Master Policy, normally called a House owners' Insurance Plan, places the lender as mortgagee as the beneficiary under the policy. As a borrower, you can request to view the terms and conditions of the policy contract.

Individual Policy

Once you own a house, it is advisable that you purchase homeowners' insurance to cover the replacement value of your home. If a mortgage exists, but the value of the property increases in keeping with the existing market, the homeowner should arrange to upgrade the sum insured so that in the event of a total loss, compensation would be adequate.

Helpful Hints

- Exercise due care in safeguarding your assets, such as your home or household contents.
- Minimize the risks of loss or damage to your home, for example, by installing security systems (including "burglar-proofing") and fire extinguishing devices.
- Carefully examine the terms and conditions of the policies of various providers before choosing an insurer that best meets your needs.

Homeowner's and Householder's Comprehensive Policy

The homeowner's comprehensive policy covers buildings while the householder's comprehensive policy covers household contents.

Insured Property

The insured property includes the actual building, walls, gates, fences, and any fixed carpets and air conditioning equipment. Any building attached to the main building that is deemed to be part of the location will also be covered by the insurance policy. Swimming pools and retaining walls are not normally included under this policy, and the homeowner must declare its existence to the insurer and set a value to be used as a "sum insured" to obtain coverage.

Insured Perils

Some of the main perils that can cause loss or damage to the insured property include:

- Fire, including underground fires, lightning bolts, explosions, and thunderbolts
- Riots, strikes, lockouts, and/or labor disturbances, and/or persons of malicious intent (this is commonly known as the riot strike and malicious damage extension)
- Aircraft or other aerial devices or any article dropped from them
- Water damage resulting from burst pipes or taps or overflowing water tanks
- Theft including burglary, house breaking, and larceny
- Impact on property by motor vehicle, horse, or cattle (must not be owned by/or in the care and control of the policyholder)
- Breakage or collapse of radio or television aerials or antennae masts; what is covered is the damage caused to the house by these items and not replacement of the aerial or antenna.
- Falling of trees or branches (covers damage to the home and not the cost of removal of trees or branches)
- Smoke
- Catastrophe perils such as earthquakes, volcanic eruptions, cyclones, windstorms, and floods

- Floods that result from other causes beside hurricanes or wind-related perils
- Collapse due to subsidence or landslip

Uninsured Perils

Some perils that can cause loss or damage to the insured property, but which are not covered under the policy include:

- War
- Radioactive and nuclear risks
- Malicious damage caused by someone lawfully on the property
- Terrorism and consequential loss.

Uninsured Perils: Useful Hints

- Insurers usually impose a policy excess of between $500 and $1000 for any claim for "riot, strike, and malicious damage" caused by someone not lawfully on the property.
- The cost of repairing the burst water line is not covered. Coverage is for damage caused by the water only.
- Policies normally include a clause which states that the building (property) must not be left unoccupied for an extended period of time, usually not more than 30 to 60 days. This clause may vary from one insurer to another.
- In the case of a theft or burglary claim, there is an excess, and compensation is confined to repairs to the building.
- Damage caused by fallen trees is covered where it is as a result of an insured peril, for example, windstorm. Policies will not cover the cost of removing fallen trees or branches or damage caused to gates and fences by fallen trees and branches if the damage is caused by you, the policyholder, or someone working under your control cutting branches or felling trees.
- Insurers may decline flood coverage under homeowner's policy if your property is situated in a flood-prone area.

- Insurers do not deem gradual cracking of a building over a period of time to be damage caused by subsidence. Damage must be sudden and accidental and may require engineering evaluation.
- Damage to your building caused by river erosion or landslide is excluded.
- Perils other than fire, lightning, explosion, thunderbolt, subterranean fire, and aircraft damage all have deductibles of varying sums or percentages of the sum insured.
- You may ask your insurance company to provide additional coverage for items not included under the basic policy. However, you should note that the premiums are usually high because of the risks that may be involved. The insurance company has the right to refuse cover if your requests are considered too risky or unreasonable.

Treatment of Excess

- For claims caused by catastrophe perils, there is normally an excess of 2% of the sum insured, with a minimum amount, whichever is greater.
- In the case of a wind-related claim, the excess may be 1% of the sum insured.
- For earthquakes, the excess is no less than 2% of the sum insured.
- For example, if the building is insured for $500,000, the catastrophe excess of 2% of the sum insured means that the insurer will pay a claim only if the damage is more than $10,000. Similarly, if the sum insured is $1 million, the policy excess would be $20,000.

Homeowner's Comprehensive Policy: Additional Coverage

Insurers generally provide additional coverage under the homeowners comprehensive policy as follows:

Public Liability

Generally, public liability insurance covers the risk of injury or damage to someone visiting your home, caused for example, by slipping on a wet floor or bumping into your glass door. As the homeowner, you may be legally liable to provide compensation to that visitor or even uninvited stranger. Limits of liability vary from one insurer to another but are normally restricted to $500,000 per event.

Alternative Accommodation

In the event that the building is damaged and becomes unfit for occupancy, the insurer will pay reasonable rent for alternative accommodation while your building is being repaired, up to a limit of 10% of the sum insured. Evidence of this payment of rent is required as insurance only compensated for loss incurred. If, however, your building is tenanted and becomes unfit for occupancy as a result of damage caused by an insured peril, the insurer will compensate you, the policyholder, up to 10% of the sum insured for the loss of rental income.

Architects' and Surveyors' Fees

Fees incurred in rebuilding following damage or destruction of the building caused by an insured peril are usually covered but limited to 10% of the sum insured. It must be noted that this may be included in the total amount insured.

Cost of Removal of Debris

The cost to demolish and remove debris when a building is damaged or destroyed will be reimbursed by the insurer up to a limit of 10% of the sum insured.

Accidental Breakage of Fixed Glass

Glass forming part of the building or fixed sanitary ware and bathroom fittings are covered under this extension to the policy. Such policy extensions are usually subject to a fixed sum per policy year.

Personal Liability

Personal liability covers the risk of injury or damage to you, the homeowner, in the insured property caused for example by slipping in your bathroom. Limits of liability vary from one insurer to another.

Average Clause and Reinstatement

There are two important conditions in the homeowner's policy that are critical regarding the minimum sum insured which is commonly referred to as the "Average Clause and Reinstatement Condition."

Average Clause

This clause penalizes the policyholder, if the property is underinsured; that is, insurers normally accept 85% (some 75%) of the current value as full insurance and consider this sum as adequate for the sum insured.

Example 1: A property valued at $500,000, but insured for $425,000 is considered to be fully insured. In the event of a claim, the average clause will not apply as the sum insured is 85% of the value ($425,000/ $500,000) and the policyholder will receive payment in full less any applicable excess.

Example 2: However, a property valued at $600,000 but insured for $425000.00 is considered to be underinsured. In this instance, the sum insured is only 71% ($425,000/$600,000) of the property and the average clause will be applied in the event of a claim.

For a claim of $50,000, the insurance company will pay (425,000 × 50,000)/600,000 = $ 35,417 less any applicable excess as the sum insured is approximately 71% and the payment of loss is reduced to the same percentage insured.

Helpful Hints

- Be familiar with the contents of your insurance policy as "average" varies from one company to another.
- The maximum payment you can receive is based on the sum insured and not property value.

Reinstatement Condition

Buildings may be insured on a reinstatement basis. Insuring a building on a reinstatement basis means that in the event that the building is destroyed or damaged, the following conditions will apply:

- The coverage represents the true replacement cost.
- The property is fully insured.
- The insurer will make the agreed payment to reinstate the damaged property.
- No deduction/depreciation for wear and tear will apply.

If the insurer is unwilling or unable to reinstate the damaged property, the reinstatement condition will not apply and the settlement of loss will take into account depreciation and wear and tear.

Householders Comprehensive Policy

Most insurers will issue combined homeowner's (covering building) and householder's (covering contents of the home) policy. The building and contents will be covered against the same perils and the same extensions wherever applicable.

House Contents include:

- Household goods and personal effects (even in the case of rental property)
- Personal effects of family members living permanently with you
- Fixtures and fittings and removable carpets and rugs.

Helpful Hints

- The perils covered under the homeowner's policy are also covered under the householder's policy.
- Insurers grant various extensions to the cover, so it is important to review policy as they vary from one insurance company to another.

Generally, if there is a break-in and several items are stolen, the damage done to the property is covered under the homeowner's policy and the loss of items under the householder's policy, subject to any applicable excess. The former loss is a damage to the property and covered under the homeowner's policy and the latter is the loss of items covered by theft under the householder's policy.

The Sum Insured

It is important that you make a detailed inventory of the contents of your home in order to arrive at a realistic sum to be insured. More often than not, buyers of insurance select a sum insured that is less than the market value of the property, which is therefore inadequate for any loss that may be incurred. Claims will therefore be subject to the application of the average clause and payment of loss will be limited by the percentage of loss insured versus the actual total value of assets. In addition, if not specifically listed, insurance companies normally place a limit of liability on valuable items at 5% of the sum insured; for example, items of jewelry, television, and electronic equipment. In most cases, the 5% limit will not cover the cost of replacing these items. ***It is important that the insured should itemize and list all assets and report them to the insurer to avoid the application of the limit of liability. Supporting invoices can be submitted, so in the event there is a loss the evidence for payment is already lodged with the insurance company. In the case of a fire it is always difficult to get the purchase invoice, for example to provide the evidence of things such as cost of the asset.***

Replacement Value

Permits the insured to receive a "new item for old" as a like item will be permitted in the event of a claim.

Helpful Hints

- You should declare any item that is valued more than 5% of the sum insured, in particular, works of art, pictures, stamp collections, and other valuables. It is important to note that insurers will limit the loss for a single item if you fail to declare it.
- One should note that unless you declare each item individually, articles of gold, silver, precious metal, or jewelry will be limited to $500 on any one item and a maximum of $2500 in total while kept on the premises of the insured property
- Television sets, video, stereo, or electronic equipment will be limited to $1000 on any one item and a maximum of $2500 in all.

Some Notable Extensions of Cover: Subject to Limits

Cash

Currency notes and stamps (but not forming part of a stamp collection) are covered against loss caused by an insured peril but there is a limit, such as $1000.

Removal of Property

Inform your insurance company (insurer) of any temporary removal of contents up to 15% of the sum insured. In addition, contents held in a bank or safe deposit box, (while it is being transported to and from the bank) will be covered by this extension.

Servants' Contents

Damage to clothing and personal effects (excluding cash) of domestic servants while in your private dwelling by any insured peril but subject to a limit, such as $2500.

Alternative Accommodation

If the building is damaged and you have to find alternative accommodation while the building is undergoing repairs, the insurer will pay for amounts actually spent up to 10% of the sum insured.

Compensation for Death

Insurers will pay for the fatal injury to you, the policyholder or spouse arising from violence caused by burglars or fire up to a limit, such as $5000.

Freezer Contents

Insurers will pay for deterioration of freezer contents up to a limit, such as $500, but the power supply must have been lost for a minimum of 12 hours.

Lost Luggage

Insurers will pay for luggage lost during private travel within the Caribbean only and there is a limit, such as $1000.

If you are dissatisfied with the settling of your insurance claim, you may consult the Office of the Financial Services Ombudsman (OFSO).

Making a Complaint

The complaint must be in writing on the prescribed form. (Forms are available at the OFSO office or can be downloaded from the OFSO website www.ofso.org.tt.) The form must be signed by the complainant and the authorized representative, if necessary. It must state the names and addresses of both the complainant and the branch of the bank or insurance company. The facts pertaining to the complaint must be supported by any relevant documents. You should also include the nature and the extent of the loss suffered and the relief being sought from the OFSO.

You should purchase insurance from registered insurance companies only. See www.central-bank.org.tt or website www.ofso.org.tt for a list of registered insurance companies.

Glossary of Terms

- *Average Clause*

    - A condition which encourages homeowners to insure their property for the correct value; you, the homeowner, will be penalized by not receiving full coverage for damages if your property is underinsured. You also would not benefit if your home is overinsured.

- *Claimant*
    - The individual who makes a claim for payment of benefits under the terms of an insurance contract
- *Excess*
    - The agreed sum or percentage of the claim which the policyholder would be required to bear before the insurance company pays out any benefits on the claim
- *Fully Insured*
    - If your property is fully insured, it means that it is covered for the current market value. Regular valuations of your property and adjusting your insurance premiums to ensure that you have adequate coverage (fully insured) are advisable.
- *Homeowner's policy and Householder's Comprehensive policy*
    - Homeowner's policy covers actual buildings whereas householder's policy provides coverage for contents.
- *Master Policy*
    - The legal contract between an insurance company and a group insurance policyholder that provides coverage for a particular group of persons
- *Reinstatement Basis*
    - Insuring your property on a reinstatement basis means that in the event of any disaster, you will be able to restore your property to its position before the damage occurred.

- *Sum Insured*
  - The maximum sum that the insurance company will pay on a claim; in other words, the sum insured is an upper limit of the funds that a claimant is eligible to receive.
- *True Replacement Cost*
  - The actual cost to repair or replace your home at current market prices

7

Home Ownership

Home ownership is one of the most important milestones in an individual's lifetime. It gives an individual a sense of independence and security and marks an important phase in adulthood. Obtaining a home may be the most valuable investment an individual will undertake in their life. There are two main avenues to home ownership—purchasing a home or building a home. The process of building a home in particular may be lengthy and winding; however, in the end it will be worth the hassle.

Legal and Other Formalities

Before entering into any contractual arrangements the prospective homeowner must complete the prequalification assessment with the financial institution of choice and then begin the process of viewing and selecting an appropriate property. This can be done by utilizing the services of a real estate agent or by directly contacting the owner of the property which you wish to purchase. The appropriateness of any property is driven by the price and preference in terms of location and size. In addition to the core considerations above, there are other criteria when selecting property, especially a first-time homeowner.

C. Sahadeo, *Financial Literacy and Money Script*,
https://doi.org/10.1007/978-3-319-77075-8_7

External factors to consider when choosing a property to purchase include:

- Price range,
- Location and size of lot/plot (square footage),
- Strong/reliable structure or foundation (material used to construct the building, the way the foundation was laid, etc.),
- Material used to build the roof,
- External finishes,
- Security/safety and type of neighborhood, and
- Access to amenities and other necessary services.

Internal factors to consider when choosing property to purchase include:

- Electrical wiring and plumbing,
- Size and quantity of rooms—bedroom and bathrooms,
- Proper internal structure, for example, inner wall and flooring,
- Signs of mold/water damage or shoddy masonry work,
- Condition of woodwork (if any) and be on the lookout for termites,
- Availability of cupboards/closets/storage space, and
- Finishing (esthetic) touches—such as molding.

Covenants: When purchasing a property, you should also ensure that you are fully aware of any restrictive covenants that are attached to the property. Restrictive covenants that you may encounter include:

- The height of the fence and the type of material that can be used
- The keeping of pets
- The noise level permitted after a particular time
- Parking
- The number of levels allowed
- The type of activities not allowed—for example, wholesale/retail business
- Rates and taxes including maintenance fees (if applicable), lease rent, water rates, and land and building (property) taxes
- If you have decided to purchase property from someone who is not the original owner, you should request a copy of the deed in which any restrictive covenants are quoted.

- In condominiums, townhouse developments, and apartment complexes, you may also have to deal with common walls/partitions and the restrictions that apply to them (e.g., breaking of walls, running of electrical wires, etc.), and common service charges or maintenance fees.

Recommendations to guide first-time homeowners in selecting a property:

- Take photos of property viewed at various angles.
- Rate the properties on a scale of 1–10 (10 being the highest) to narrow the selections.
- Make detailed notes while viewing properties. Highlight the pros and the cons.
- View the top three or four selections at least another time before making a decision.
- View property during the daytime so that it is easier to identify flaws.
- Research the area in which the property is located and speak to residents in and around the area to learn of any possible drawbacks.
- Take time when viewing the property.
- Obtain all relevant information from the real estate agent or vendor of the property and verify that the vendor is in fact the owner of the property.

It is important to understand the major difference between registered and unregistered (old law) land. Many countries in the Caribbean have begun the process of registration of title which has been introduced by statutes in most Commonwealth Caribbean jurisdictions. The main aim is to simplify conveyancing; but more importantly, it ensures that a purchaser or mortgagee dealing with the registered proprietor of title of land will obtain an absolute and indefeasible title. Once land has been registered under the Act, a certificate of title is issued for it and is kept at the Registrar/Office of Titles. A counterpart to the original (known as the duplicate certificate of title) is also issued and is kept by the owner of property as his/her proof of ownership. It is this same duplicate which is usually held by a mortgage institution when someone borrows money and uses their property as security for the loan. One of the main advantages of this system is that all transactions involving the property are always reflected on the certificate of title for the property.

With respect to unregistered land, however, no such certificate of title is available. An owner of unregistered land has a deed, which shows that he/she is the owner. In order to sell or mortgage the property a search must be conducted which involves the tracing of several documents. Title must be traced from the root of title right down to the vendor. The attorney commissions a search clerk to prepare an abstract of title, which is a summary of the documents and events by which any dispositions of the property have been made during the period for which title has to be shown.

A contract for sale of land must be construed as containing the following implied terms:

(a) The vendor has a good and marketable title to the land.
(b) The vendor would deliver an abstract of title to the purchaser within a reasonable time from the date of contract.
(c) Both vendor and purchaser would proceed to completion within a reasonable period of time from the contract date.

In the sale of unregistered land, the vendor has a twofold duty with respect to the title of the property he is selling. First he must disclose any latent defects to title and secondly he is obliged to "*make a good title to the whole legal and equitable interest in the freehold land free from encumbrances and to prove that fact.*" This puts the onus on the purchaser's attorney to search the title in the Registry, and while the onus remains on the vendor to produce a proper title, in reality the purchaser's attorney is the one who confirms whether the title is good or not.

Good Root of Title

Documents that would serve as a good root of title for the purpose of a sale in the order of strength are:

1. a legal mortgage,
2. a conveyance of sale, and
3. specific device in a will.

Therefore the purchaser's attorney must be able to trace the title starting with a good root of title at least 20 years old. Conveyancers use the word title to mean ownership, the vendor's right to the property and evidence supporting the claim to ownership. Section 5 of the Conveyancing and Law of Property Act Chapter 56:01 (Trinidad and Tobago) states that 20 years shall be the period of commencement of the title which a purchaser may require. Title must commence with a document at least 20 years and traced from the root of title right down to the vendor.

In Barbados, the system used for buying and selling real property is modeled largely after the old English system. However the unregistered system is still predominant but there are some areas which use the registered system for sale of land. Similarly under an agreement for the sale of land in Barbados, a vendor is required to show to the purchaser good title to the land being sold. Under the Law of Property Act Chapter 236 ("the Act") (Barbados), the time limit on the history of how the land came to be owned by the vendor, which he is required to show to a purchaser, is 20 years.

The key parties involved in the sale of a property include:

The vendor—the individual selling the property
The prospective homeowner—the intended purchaser of the property
The financial institution—institutional financing for the purchase of the property with a mortgage
The guarantor—in certain circumstances where the purchaser's income is inadequate to satisfy the Loan-to-Value (LTV) ratio, an additional party, a guarantor, is included so that in the event the prospective homeowner reneges on the agreement the person who guarantees the loan will be called upon to service the loan.

The vendor has an obligation to provide all evidence not available at the Registry. Events such as marriage or death are sufficiently proved by production of certified copies of appropriate certificates. Grants of representation must be supported by corresponding certified death certificate. Provided the evidence requested in the various requisitions are adequate to prove title, then the purchaser must proceed to complete the sale. On the other hand the purchaser is entitled to rescind the contract if certain information is not forthcoming. However the rescission would have to be founded on the vendor's inability to meet a substantial objection to title, not some minor or trivial defect. The purchaser is limited to the return of the deposit, without costs or interest (unless the vendor is tardy in repaying it.)

The purchasing of property involves a series of transactions which include identification of the property, prequalification assessment, purchase agreement, financing the purchase price usually by a mortgage, and the preparation of a deed of conveyance and deed of mortgage.

The Prequalification Assessment Most prospective homeowners would not have the funds to purchase a home. However they would need to have at least the funds for the down payment (at least 10%) and closing costs. The buyer would need to finance any shortfall in funds that is the difference between the purchase price, the approved loan, closing costs, and funds personally held. Prior to entering into an agreement to purchase property the purchaser needs to calculate the maximum amount of loan he qualifies for based on his present circumstances. Albeit many financial institutions have models for calculating this online, visits should be made to selected financial institutions to get confirmation on the amount of mortgage loan for which the buyer qualifies. This is called a prequalification assessment.

Financial institutions require the following information to complete the pre-qualification assessment:

(i) **Current income**: This is required to compute the amount of mortgage an individual may qualify for. The financial institution would need to know whether the person is permanently employed or on contract employment, and whether the person is employed full-time or part-time. Financial institutions need proof of income as evidenced by a recent job letter or pay slip and are mostly interested in basic remuneration and not overtime or commission payment since the latter is not constant. Individuals who are self-employed may find it difficult to provide proof of current income if they do not keep proper records/accounts of their business. However, in order for their application to be considered, the business must be a going concern and fully operational and would request copies of bank statements as evidence of income.

(ii) **Place of employment**: The place of employment can add credibility to the application where the organization has prominence in the business community and offers job security for its employees.

(iii) **Monthly (fixed) expenses**: These expenses include rent, utility bills, loan payments, hire purchase installments, and so on. This information is used in the calculation of the debt service ratio.

(iv) **Occasional (variable) expenses**: These expenses are discretionary and include such expenses as entertainment, cinema, restaurants, and vacation.

(v) **Debt:** The borrower is required to disclose all debt obligations. This can take the form of outstanding loans for a vehicle, household appliances, and education. This would also be used in calculating the debt service ratio.

(vi) **Assets:** These include land, vehicles, investments, and cash in bank/financial institutions. This information is needed to ensure an applicant has enough/some additional collateral to secure the mortgage loan.

(vii) **Credit history:** A credit history is done for all applications for loans as this provides important information regarding the applicant's debt servicing and loan repayment history. A credit report is a record of the borrower's credit history from a number of sources, including banks, credit card companies, and collection agencies and reflects the applicant's ability to repay a loan. Credit history is a critical factor used in credit rating and is employed by lending institutions as a qualifier for a loan. In addition to this information, the financial institution will compute the maximum loan amount for which the borrower may qualify and recommends the loan products or financing options that may be best suited to the applicant. The prequalification assessment is considered to be the initial step in the acquiring of a mortgage loan. It is the start of a relationship with the financial institution of your choice

(viii) **Loan-to-Value Ratio (LTV):** The financial institutions use the financial data provided to calculate the LTV. The latter is a factor the lending company will use to determine the amount of mortgage the applicant qualifies for. The LTV ratio describes the relationship between the proposed loan and the value of the property. The higher the ratio, the higher the risk to the lender. Generally, most mortgage providers will lend between 75% and 90% of the cost or value of the property. In such instances the purchaser is required to fund the balance of the purchase price of the property. Government lending agencies sometimes allow 100% financing for lower-income families.

The borrower is required to fund the residual amount of the cost of the property—that is the amount not financed by the mortgage. Therefore the higher the LTV ratio, the smaller the personal funding requirement, and the lower the LTV ratio, the higher the personal funding requirement. For example, assume you intend to buy a home for $1,000,000. You will qualify for a mortgage loan of $900,000 if your LTV ratio is 90% and for a mortgage loan of $800,000 if your LTV ratio is 80%. In the first instance you are required to contribute $100,000 toward the purchase of the property and in the second instance your contribution will be $200,000. The mortgage provider will only lend in excess of the LTV ratio in rare circumstances and would also require additional security such as mortgage indemnity insurance.

The purchasing agreement or **agreement for sale** is the first contract between the vendor and purchaser. A purchase agreement contains the following:

- The name of the owner (vendor);
- The name of the purchaser;
- The address and size of the property being purchased;
- The purchase/sale price; and
- The down payment (normally 10% of purchase price) and terms for the payment of the balance (usually 90 days from the signing of the agreement).

The purchaser should always seek professional legal advice before signing the purchase agreement. This agreement must be signed by:

- The owner (vendor) or his agent;
- The purchaser; and
- Witnesses to the signatures.

It is advisable for the parties to the purchase agreement to make provisions for any monies arising from the transaction to be held in escrow. Escrow refers to monies held by a third party (usually an attorney), on behalf of the vendor and purchaser. The cash and deeds should be held in escrow until the lending institution receives the appropriate written or oral instructions or until obligations have been fulfilled. When the purchaser makes the down payment, these funds should be held by the attorney and not paid directly to the seller until proper title to the property has been established. This protects the buyer's down payment in the event that there is problem with the title or some other issue that prevents the transaction from being completed.

A receipt must be provided for any money paid, particularly for the down payment made to the vendor. It is also advisable that these payments should not be in cash. Two legal documents, that is, the deed of conveyance or memorandum of transfer (for registered land) and the deed of mortgage are normally prepared consecutively. Most financial institutions have a panel of attorneys which must be used in the preparation of deeds. The fees incurred, however, may be less if one attorney prepares both deeds.

When signing the purchase agreement the buyer should ensure that the vendor is the same as the person named as the owner in the existing title deed. All named owners in the title deed must also be named as vendors in the agreement. The loan will be based on either the valuation or purchase price of the property, whichever is lower. Before the release of funds for payment of property the attorney must ensure that all liens on the property have been satisfied. The agreement must contain a clause that would allow funds to be held in escrow by an independent agreed third party so that the purchaser would be able to retrieve funds in the event of an untoward occurrence. There are many fraudulent activities or practices in the conveyancing of land and the purchaser must be ever aware of the phrase "buyer beware" as the buyer assumes the risk.

Applying for a Mortgage Loan: The financial institution would require the following:

Personal Information

- Evidence of nationality (identification card, driver's permit, or passport);
- Evidence of income (job letter and pay slip);
- Statements of loans;
- Statements of savings; and
- Evidence of current address (copy of utility bill).

The Purchasing of property requires the following:

- Title deed or lease from the vendor—This is a legal document to prove the ownership of a property.

- Survey plan—This is a drawing of the boundaries and any physical objects on the property. This plan is prepared and signed by a licensed surveyor.
- Completion certificate (required for properties less than four years old)—This document states that the house or building has been successfully constructed in accordance with approved plans. The certificate is issued by the Office of the Local Regional Authority.
- Property (Land and Building) tax receipt—Property cannot be transferred unless it is free of any liens and all taxes must be current and up to date. This receipt confirms that the tax payments on the property are up to date and there are no pending claims by the relevant authority.
- Water and Sewage Authority clearance certificate—Like land and building taxes, the receipt provides confirmation that there are no outstanding payments due on the property.
- Valuation report—This report provides the fair market value of the property if it were to be sold in the open market. It details the general condition of the building, the size of the total house and land, and recommended insurable value of the property.

Purchasing Land Only

The documentation required for the purchase of land is the same as for the purchase of a house except that the land and building tax receipt will be replaced by a land tax receipt only.

Purchasing a Townhouse or Condominium

A townhouse/condominium development has general areas which are not detailed in the deed of conveyance of the individual unit. This general area is held in the name of a holding company, and as a homeowner, you also become a co-owner of this company. An original share certificate is issued to the owner of each unit.

Costs and Fees in Buying Property

It is important that the buyer knows all the cost and fees incurred in buying a property. By knowing this figure the buyer can budget and save for the down payment and other fees. In order for the mortgage application to be processed, a number of documents are required by the financial institution. Some of the documents and their respective fees are outlined below:

1. *Credit Check Report*
   The financial institution will notify the card holder that the information will be sent to a credit checking institution to receive a history of all credit facilities that the proposed borrower has been granted in order to determine his or her credit worthiness. This institution will provide a status report on the borrower's credit history. The applicant bears this cost.
2. *Valuation Report Fee*
   A valuation report is a document outlining the current value of a property in the market based on many factors including location, price, and size. The fee for this report varies from 1/4th of 1% to 1/3rd of 1% of the value of the property being purchased or assessed, in addition to Value Added Tax (VAT) and incidentals.

Example: Calculation of fees for valuation report based on property valued at $400, 000 and at the rate of 1/4% and 1/3%

$$\text{Valuation fees}: \$400{,}000 \times 1/4 \times 1\% = \$1000$$

$$\text{Valuation fees}: \$400{,}000 \times 1/3 \times 1\% = \$1333.33$$

3. *Loan Processing Fee*
   This is calculated as a percentage of the loan amount and is usually 1–1.5% of the amount loaned. In some instances, the financial institution has a flat fee. This fee can be negotiated.

4. *Legal and Other Fees*

These are a significant part of the total cost incurred in purchasing a property. Most prospective homeowners are unaware of these fees and have difficulty financing these unbudgeted costs.

The fees that are generally incurred in purchasing and financing a home are as follows:

- Search fees;
- Stamp duty for the deed of conveyance;
- Stamp duty for the deed of mortgage;
- Attorneys' fees for preparation of the deed of conveyance;
- Attorneys' fees for preparation of the deed of mortgage;
- Valuation fees

Stamp duty is a mandatory tax payable to the Board of Inland Revenue levied on the instrument that effects a conveyance or mortgage. A failure to pay stamp duty or the payment of the incorrect amount will render the instrument inadmissible as evidence in a court. In practice, the Registry will not accept an instrument for registration unless it has been duly stamped. If the value of residential land is $850,000.00 or less, there is no stamp duty payable on the instrument (Tables 7.1, 7.2, and 7.3).

For purchases of land only, 0.4% of the amount is secured by the mortgage.

The attorneys' fees are charged for the preparation of conveyances, transfers, and mortgages. These are based on the statutory scales in the Attorneys-at-Law (Remuneration) (Non-Contentious Business) Rules

Table 7.1 The stamp duty on residential land with house thereon

Property value	Stamp duty payable (%)
Up to $850,000	Exempt
For the next $400,000 ($850,000–$1,250,000)	3%
For the next $500,000 ($1,250,000–$1,750,000)	5% on the amount exceeding $1,250,000 plus $12,000
Over $1,750,000	7.5% on amount exceeding $1,750,000 plus $37,000

Table 7.2 The stamp duty on residential land only

Property value	Stamp duty payable (%)
Less than $450,000	Exempt
$450,000–$650,000	2%
For the next $200,000	5% on amount exceeding $650,000 plus $4000
For every dollar in excess of $850,000 thereafter	7% on amount exceeding $850,000 plus $14,000

Table 7.3 Stamp duty payable on mortgages: residential property (with a house thereon)

Amount of loan	Stamp duty payable(%)
If borrowing less than $850,000	Exempt
If borrowing less than $850,000 but more than the purchase price	0.4% on amount in excess of purchase price
If borrowing more than $850,000 but less than purchase price	0.2% of the whole
If borrowing more than $850,000 and more than purchase price	0.2% on purchase price plus 0.4% on amount exceeding purchase price

1997 (Legal Notice #77 of 1997) and different rates apply for conveyancing transactions under the Common Law and under the Real Property Act (the "RPA"). Attorneys' fees for the preparation of these instruments are based on the value of the consideration (or in the case of a gift, the value of the property being conveyed). In the case of a mortgage the attorneys' fees are charged on the amount secured. However, if both a Common Law conveyance and mortgage are completed at the same time and prepared by the same attorney-at-law, the full-scale fee for conveyances shall be charged on the conveyance calculated on the consideration and one-half of the fee for mortgages shall be charged on the mortgage, calculated on the amount secured (Tables 7.4, 7.5, and 7.6).

When you have repaid your mortgage in full, you will receive written notification from the relevant financial institution advising you of the same. You should take a copy of your deed of mortgage to your attorney or an attorney on the panel of attorneys of the financial institution in order to request your deed of release. If you fail to secure your deed of release the financial institution will continue to hold your property as security and this will affect your ability to transfer your property free from encumbrances (Tables 7.7 and 7.8).

Table 7.4 Scale of attorneys' fees for common law conveyances and mortgages

Value of the property conveyed/consideration	Stamp duty payable (%)	
0–$100,000	1.50%	With a minimum fee of $400
$100,000–$500,000	0.75%	On amount exceeding $100,000 plus $1500
$500,000–$20,000,000	0.50%	On amount exceeding $500,000 plus $4500
Over $20,000,000		At the attorney's discretion having regard to the complexity of the transaction, the skill, labor, specialized knowledge involved, the number and importance of the documents prepared, and the place where and circumstances in which the business or any part thereof is transacted

Table 7.5 Scale of attorney's fees for transfers and mortgages under the Real Property Act

Value of property conveyed/ consideration	Stamp duty payable (%)
0–$25,000	$500
Over $25,000	$500 for the first $25,000 of the consideration and $30 for every $5000 or part thereof in excess of $25,000.00 (to calculate deduct 25,000, divide the difference by $5000, multiply by $30 then add $500)

Table 7.6 Sample computation of attorneys' fees and stamp duty for the conveyance of residential property

Value of consideration	Attorneys' fees	Stamp duty	Attorneys' fees under the RPA
$750,000	$5750	Exempt	$4850
$1,000,000	$7000	$4500	$6350
$1,500,000	$9500	$24,500	$9350
$2,000,000	$12,000	$55,750	$12,350
$3,000,000	$17,000	$130,750	$18,350

Table 7.7 Attorneys' fees for the deed of release

Property value	Rates/fee charged
Not exceeding $25,000	$250
Exceeding $25,000	$250.00 for the first $25,000.00 and $15.00 for every $5000.00 or part thereof of the amount in excess of $25,000.00 up to a maximum fee of $10,000.00

Table 7.8 Sample computation of legal fees, stamp duty, and other fees for preparation of deeds of conveyance and mortgages (old law) for the following values

	House and land (old law)	Mortgage (90%)	House and land (old law)	Mortgage (80%)
Purchase price	**$1,000,000**	**$900,000 ($1,000,000 × 90%)**	**$1,500,000**	**$1,200,000 ($1,500,000 × 80%)**
Legal fees	$7000	$3250	$9500	$4000
VAT	$875	$406	$1188	$500
Stamp duty (based on the consideration/sum borrowed)	$4500	$1800	$24,500	$2400
Registration	$100	$100	$100	$100
Disbursements approx.	$1600	$600	$1600	$600

Other Key Factors

It is important that you be aware of the following factors that are relevant to the granting of mortgage loans, in order to avoid unnecessary wasting of time and costs.

1. Who qualifies for mortgage loans in Trinidad and Tobago?
2. Size of the loan

   - Personal income, debt, credit history, and age will determine the quantum that can be borrowed and also the period of the loan.

3. Debt service ratio

   - Generally, the mortgage installment should not exceed one-third of gross monthly income. Additionally, the mortgage installment together with any other loan commitments should not exceed 40% of the gross monthly income.

4. Select wisely

   - Decide whether you are going to purchase house and land or purchase land and construct a home.
   - Identify a property which you can afford.
   - Remember property is all about "Location! Location! Location!"

Assessment of Guarantors

A guarantor is a person or corporation who guarantees payment by another and becomes a co-endorser and assumes liability in the event of default. Many financial institutions do not use guarantors as financial support in mortgage loans. Prospective borrowers/homeowners are expected to qualify for a mortgage facility based on their financial well-being. There are, however, exceptions when the inclusion of a guarantor is allowed.

In those circumstances, the would-be guarantor is assessed on the same basis as the borrower:

- Income verification must be provided, that is, job letters, salary slips, and so on.
- All existing liabilities must be declared.
- Record of savings and evidence of assets must be provided.
- Credit checks are also carried out to determine credit worthiness.

For prospective guarantors, the bank recommends an independent legal counsel be obtained so that they are fully aware of their obligations under the mortgage. This is now mandatory as there is a potential conflict of interest if an external party has not ensured the guarantor was not maneuvered to sign to the benefit of the bank in the event of default of the borrower. The guarantor must be mindful that if the borrower defaults in his payments the guarantor would be called upon to do so!

Deed of Conveyance

The deed of conveyance transfers ownership from the previous owner to purchaser and must be prepared prior to the preparation of the deed of mortgage. The deed of mortgage transfers ownership to the financial institution, the mortgagee. The financial institution will disburse funds once the attorney has confirmed that the title is good (proper root of title), and the deed of conveyance and the deed of mortgage are executed. The attorney will then register the deeds and provide the purchaser with a copy.

Finally, the return of ownership form is prepared by the attorney. This serves to inform the District Revenue Office that you now own the property. The new owner is responsible for ensuring that this process is completed in order to receive the certificate of assessment for payment of water and sewerage rates and land and building taxes.

Finalization of the Mortgage Contract

Once the prospective buyer satisfies the stringent qualifying measures for the mortgage loan and adequacy of the security offered is ascertained, the offer of the mortgage loan is made and on acceptance, the financial institution will instruct its attorney to conduct the relevant title search on the property which is to be mortgaged and prepare the relevant documents. A title search will show all encumbrances, liens, judgments, or prior mortgages. As a caution, vendors and prospective mortgagors should also search for judgments. Once the title is good, the relevant deeds are prepared. Some elements of the important terms and conditions contained in the mortgage include:

- The parties to the mortgage;
- Description and location of the property being mortgaged;
- The terms of repayment;
- The interest rate and whether it is fixed or variable;
- The date on which monthly installments are due; and
- Penalties for late payment or early repayment.

A mortgage deed is a document whereby the owner of a property (mortgagor) transfers an interest in real estate to a lending institution (mortgagee) for the purpose of providing a mortgage loan. It is the evidence of the interest transferred to the mortgage holder. It is a written instrument that creates a claim or lien upon real estate as security for the payment of a specified debt. Given the high cost of obtaining a home, most people fund the purchase and financing of their home from borrowings from a financial institution which is securitized by way of a mortgage of the said property. This instrument can be quite long and intimidating.

The mortgage deed includes:

- The parties to the mortgage—the lending institution, borrower, guarantor (if there is one);
- Agreement date;

- The amount being borrowed;
- The rate of interest and terms of repayment (including rules pertaining to prepayment);
- Clauses which govern the manner in which the property should be kept;
- Clauses that allow officers of the lending institution to visit the property to ensure that it is being maintained (The property is being held by the lending institution as security for the funds you borrowed and as such they will want to ensure that the property is not being allowed to deteriorate);
- Requirement for all rates and taxes to be kept up to date and for the property to be adequately insured. The borrower will be required to provide proof that all rates and taxes are kept up to date and that the property is adequately insured and amounts for which the property should be insured.
- The procedure that will be followed in the event of foreclosure.

Before signing the mortgage deed the following should be checked for agreed terms and accuracy:

- The spelling of full name as detailed in the identification used,
- Current mailing address,
- The amount being borrowed,
- The interest rate, and
- The terms of the loan.

A mortgage loan can be granted at a fixed, variable, or adjustable rate.

A fixed rate mortgage is characterized by an interest rate that is constant for the duration of the mortgage. Most mortgages however have a variable rate of interest, but the mortgage deed must stipulate the terms and conditions or circumstances whereby the rate of interest will be changed at any time during the life of the mortgage. An adjustable rate mortgage has an interest rate that can periodically change based on an index which is tied to the cost of borrowing to the financial institution. The advantage of a fixed rate mortgage is that the payment is fixed and the borrower is protected against future increases in market interest rates.

Adjustable rate mortgage usually commences at a lower interest rate than fixed rate mortgages; thus the borrower can qualify for a larger mortgage; also this type of mortgage benefits the borrower in a market where interest rates are reducing.

Mortgage loan facilities can be accessed at financial institutions for the purchase of a house and/or land. A first-time home owner also has access to the preferential mortgage rates that the government has in place to facilitate home ownership. The acquisition of a home requires a large capital outlay and most persons would require funding. Financial institutions provide funding using the property as security by an instrument called a deed of mortgage. However the lending company will have to evaluate the mortgage application and the quantum of loan that the applicant qualifies for based on the applicant's gross monthly income (either singly or jointly), age of the applicant, the level of indebtedness (debt service ratio), and credit history.

Generally, the monthly mortgage payment should not exceed one-third of the gross monthly income. For example, the maximum installment for a person with monthly income of $5000.00 will be 1/3 × $5000.00 or $1666.67.

The maximum period of the mortgage (length of loan) is normally 30 years or the period up to the applicant's 60th birthday, whichever comes first. The next consideration is the level of indebtedness as this is used to compute the debt service ratio. The higher the level of debt the borrower has, the lower the amount of funding available to finance the purchase of the property. This is because the general policy is that the monthly debt repayment (including the mortgage installment) should not exceed 40% of monthly income. Most interest rates vary somewhat across financial institutions. The lowest rates under the approved Mortgage Company Programme are currently offered by the Trinidad and Tobago Mortgage Finance Company (TTMF) that is 2% per annum for mortgages up to $1,000,000 for income less than $14,000 and property with values less than $1,000,000.

It is important to note that the mortgage rate for lending institutions vary depending on the general movement in interest rates. This is so because in principle, the mortgage rate is a variable rate; it can move with changes in interest rates. If interest rates register a sustained increase, it is possible that lending institutions will increase the interest rate on a variable rate mortgage. It is important to shop around and visit as many financial institutions as possible for a mortgage that provides the best terms and conditions suitable to your situation.

If you are a salaried worker, you must be able to provide proof of your total monthly income in the form of a job letter and your most recent pay slip. Variable income such as overtime, acting allowances, and bonuses are not usually considered part of your gross income. It is advisable that the maximum monthly mortgage installment should not exceed 30% of gross monthly basic income. If the buyer is self-employed, the following will be required:

- Bank statements for a minimum of the last two years;
- Financial statements for a minimum of the last three years; and
- Tax returns for the same period.

Foreclosure

This can be defined as the legal process by which a person's right to a property is terminated, usually because the borrower has failed to meet the covenants contained in the mortgage. The major breach is the non-monthly payment of the loan by the borrower who may be unable to meet the mortgage payment due to a change in his financial situation. The mortgage deed gives the financial institution the power for the mortgagee to foreclose for breach of any covenant detailed in the mortgage. Some common financial situations that may lead to foreclosure can include becoming unemployed, a reduction in earnings, or experiencing a change in your marital status (e.g., separation, divorce, or death of one party).

Different strategies can be implemented to avoid or reduce the likelihood of foreclosure. It is recommended that all persons with debt in particular establish an emergency fund. This type of fund would allow you to weather the storm and meet financial obligations, in the event of the occurrence of any of the aforementioned situations. Additional techniques to avoid foreclosure on your property may include:

- Mortgage installment protection;
- Reducing expenditure by making and adhering to a strict budget;
- Supplementing your income by getting a second job or through utilizing your skills to generate additional income; and
- Downsizing to a property for which the payments would be more affordable.

Regardless of the situation, it is recommended that you keep the mortgagee (financial institution) informed. This could result in a renegotiated arrangement or plan being specifically structured thereby avoiding the challenges associated with foreclosure.

Mortgage Market Guideline

The purchase of a home is one of the largest and most important investments that the average individual will undertake during her/his lifetime. Most individuals purchase a home by borrowing from a bank or other mortgage provider. Given the mortgage repayment is usually a substantial part of an individual's income, normally 35% of total income and is long term in nature, it is important that the mortgagor (i.e., the borrower) clearly understands the terms and conditions of the mortgage.

Information compiled by the Central Bank suggests that many consumers are not well informed about key aspects of their mortgage contracts. Indeed, several customers do not pay sufficient attention to the type of the mortgage facility that they own (fixed, variable, or adjustable rate), the additional fees and charges that they need to pay, and most importantly when, why, and how their mortgage rates change.

In an effort to improve the disclosure and transparency in the local residential mortgage market, the CBTT in consultation with Bankers' Association of Trinidad and Tobago (BATT), has introduced the "Residential Real Estate Mortgage Market Guidelines" in September 14, 2011. The scope of this guideline includes all new and existing residential real estate mortgages granted by licensees. The guideline contains two important features: the requirement for licensees to provide a "Disclosure Statement" to customers and the introduction of a "Mortgage Market Reference Rate."

The Disclosure Statement: This is designed to summarize the pertinent facts of the mortgage contract in an easy-to-read and understandable format. This statement will provide important information about the mortgage contract such as:

- The type of mortgage—that is fixed, variable, or adjustable;
- The interest rate that is applied to your mortgage;
- When your mortgage interest rate is expected to be reviewed and/or changed;
- The mortgage market reference rate;
- The margin applied by the bank to your mortgage;
- How your mortgage payments will be split between principal and interest (the amortization schedule); and
- The various charges and fees which form part of your mortgage contract.

The Mortgage Market Reference Rate (MMRR)

The MMRR is an interest rate benchmark against which mortgages are to be priced and re-priced and will be announced by the Central Bank on a quarterly basis. The MMRR is computed by the Central Bank based on information on commercial banks' funding costs and yields on applicable treasury bonds. The mortgage rate will be based on the MMRR plus the margin charged by your bank.

The MMRR will make one aware of changing conditions in the mortgage market. This will enable the borrower to better determine when and why the mortgage is likely to change. The mortgage rate usually changes when the MMRR changes, and for mortgages with variable interest rates, reference is made to the MMRR as the basis for increase in the interest rate in the deed of mortgage. If the MMRR declines, the borrower should benefit from lower mortgage rates provided it is a variable rate mortgage or an adjustable rate mortgage. Alternatively if the MMRR rises, the mortgage rate could rise at the option of the bank.

Banks should provide the borrower with a disclosure statement which will contain the main elements of the mortgage contract in an easy-to-read and understandable format. This disclosure must be accompanied by an amortization schedule for the mortgage in which the monthly installments are shown split between principal and interest payments. The amortization schedule details the principal and interest element in each installment.

The Central Bank has introduced these Guidelines because there was increasing evidence that customers were not fully aware of some of the key aspects of their mortgage contracts. The intent of this Guideline is to ensure that customers are better informed about the terms and conditions of their mortgage contracts. The Guideline came into effect on December 1, 2011, for new mortgages and March 1, 2012, for existing mortgages.

Existing mortgage holders are delayed from moving to the new MMRR regime because current mortgage contracts mandate that customers be given prior notice before their mortgage rates are adjusted. This period of notice ranges between one to three months depending on your mortgage contract. The Guideline is not applicable to mortgages granted under special housing arrangements by the Trinidad and Tobago Mortgage Finance Company (TTMF) as the government has put in place special housing programs to assist vulnerable groups in society.

If interest rates rise rapidly, there are two main mechanisms to protect customers. Firstly, licensees have the option not to increase mortgage rates even if the MMRR is rising. Secondly, the Guideline states that over any three-year period, the mortgage rate can increase by a maximum of 350 basis points (1/100 of one percentage point) or by the increase in the Central Bank's "Repo rate," whichever is larger. Therefore, the Guideline places a limit on the size of increase in the mortgage rate over any three-year period.

The Guidelines will not result in a lower monthly payment rate. This depends on a number of factors including how the MMRR moves and how your risks are assessed by your bank. Generally lump-sum payments can be made toward the mortgage provided it is a term or condition of the contract. Information on the Guideline can be obtained from your banker as well as the website of the CBTT, National-financial Literacy Program (NFLP), and the Bankers' Association of Trinidad & Tobago (BATT) via the following links:

http://www.central-bank.org.tt/content/legislation-guidelines-and-letters-0
http://www.national-financialliteracy.org.tt
Residential%20Real%20Estate%*20 Mortgage*%20Market%*20 Guideline*.pdf http://www.batt.org.tt/articles/residential-mortgage-guidelines.html

Possible Causes for Delay in Completion of a Mortgage Transaction

There are a number of issues that can prolong a mortgage transaction; the following are some of the events that can occur:

- Title Issues—On receipt of instruction for preparation of deeds the attorney must ensure the title search of the property begins immediately. The length of time for the searches to be completed will vary depending on whether title to the property falls under Common Law or under the provisions of the Real Property Act (RPA). A title search of the property under the RPA can usually be completed within two days. However, locating the certificate of title can take considerably longer. An average title search may be completed within 14 days.
- In a mortgage transaction where the title is good, delays may occur for one or more of the following reasons:
  - There is an existing mortgage on record—This can delay the transaction as the attorneys must ensure that a release of this mortgage has been effected.

- A judgment is discovered—A judgment operates like a charge over the property of the person against whom it is registered. If you purchase property from someone with a judgment registered against him or her, you acquire the property and all property-related debts of the previous owner.
- A lis pendens is discovered—This gives notice of a High Court action that may affect the property.
- The certificate of title is missing.
- The land and building tax receipt is not in the name of the vendor.
- There exist discrepancies between assessment numbers stated on land and building taxes (property tax) and water rate receipts.
- A party to the transaction cannot be located.
- A previous owner is now deceased—Depending on the manner of ownership of the property, the vendor would have to provide the death certificate or a grant of probate/letters of administration.

• In some transactions a proper root of title cannot be established. This can cause significant and costly delays in the following circumstances:

  - Someone acquires a property by a deed of gift, but proper transfer of title was not done. In such an instance a deed of rectification will have to be done.
  - A person has ownership together with a minor (someone under the age of 18). This could prevent such a person from selling or doing anything with the property until the minor becomes of age. A court order showing that the action to be taken is for the benefit of the minor could be used to facilitate transactions.
  - Incorrectly spelt names, change of names, or aliases not reflected on the title deed will pose problems and will require the vendor to prepare a deed of rectification prior to the transfer.
  - Land subdivided from a larger parcel—A proper root of title must be seen for the original parcel and the subdivision should have been approved by Lands and Survey department.
  - Occupation of a property (state or private lands) without interruption for 16 or more years could give rise to rights by the occupants, according to the Real Property Limitation Act Chapter 56:03.

Declaration of Financial Obligations

Accurate and complete information should be provided regarding the applicant's financial commitments. All financial obligations, regardless of how minimal they may appear, must be declared. Your monthly mortgage installment, in addition to your other debt obligations, generally should not exceed 40% of total monthly income (Total Debt Service Ratio).

These additional debt obligations include:

- Credit card loans
- Hire purchase loans
- Credit union loans
- Motor vehicle loans
- Alimony
- Child maintenance payments
- Any other commitments.

Debt Service Ratio (DSR)

The Debt Service Ratio (DSR) is a guide used by lending institutions to determine the borrowers' ability to meet their monthly installments without undue financial hardship or strain. In calculating the DSR, the financial institution would include payments on all debt commitments, including monthly costs associated with the homeownership (e.g., maintenance costs), as a percentage of the borrower(s) total monthly income. Generally for mortgage lending, the financial institutions work with a debt service ratio of 40%.

The Debt Service Ratio is determined by the following formula:

Monthly Mortgage Installment + Other Monthly Debt Commitments
+[(Annual Property Tax + Home Owners Insurance Premium
+Maintenance Fees if applicable) / 12] / Gross Monthly Income

For example, Mr. and Mrs. Smith are interested in purchasing a town-house in a gated community. While their proposed monthly mortgage installment is $3000, the Smiths are required to pay monthly maintenance fees of $500 to the management company of the gated community, $1500 on a car loan, and $350 on their credit card. As new owners of the town house, they will also be required to pay annually land and building taxes of $500 and property insurance of $2000. As a security officer and a school teacher, the Smiths' gross combined monthly salary is $15,000.

The Debt Service Ratio (DSR) for Mr. & Mrs. Smith is calculated as follows:

$$\$3000 + \$500 + \$1500 + \$350 \\ + [\$500 + \$2000 / 12] \div \$15000 = 37.05\%$$

Mr. and Mrs. Smith would qualify for the stipulated loan as the debt service ratio is less than 40%. In addition the applicant must provide evidence of the availability of funds for the down payment (the buyer's contribution to the purchase of the property) and fees and costs involved in the completion of the mortgage transaction.

Joint Applications

When applying for a mortgage with other parties, all persons involved must be fully aware of their obligations under the terms of the mortgage deed. In the event that a mortgage is granted to joint applicants, all parties are jointly and severally liable under the mortgage deed. This applies regardless of the relationship among the parties, whether husband and wife, parent and child, siblings (brother and sister), or business partners.

When a child enters into a mortgage agreement with a parent, he must be made fully aware of the impact of that decision on his debt service ratio as it could possibly prevent him from obtaining a mortgage to finance the purchase of his own home or loss of preferential first-time homeowner benefits. The bank must ensure that all parties get independent legal advice owing to potential conflict of interest.

The purchasing of a home may be the biggest investment one may make in a lifetime. Initially one has a little equity unless a large down payment is made but as one makes monthly mortgage payments, the homeowner will gradually acquire greater equity in the property. Importantly property tends to increase in value over time. As with all investments, there is risk that the mortgagee can foreclose if there is a default in payments of the loan, but usually some time can be negotiated if there is a temporary loss of income.

Contract Details

When either buying or building a home there are several contracts and it is important that all parties to the contract read and get legal and financial advice where necessary. Some possible contracts you may have to sign (execute) are as follows (Table 7.9):

Table 7.9 Contracts to sign/execute

Document/ instrument	Description	Parties involved
Purchase agreement	Agreement between the purchaser and seller detailing the terms including the maximum time (normally 90 days) for settlement of balance or final payment	Vendor/agent and purchaser
Mortgage agreement	Between the financial institution and the purchaser outlining the total sum to be borrowed, the rate of interest, and the repayment terms and covenats	Lending institution and purchaser/ mortgagor
Deed of conveyance	Purchase price, schedule defining description of property, any right of way, restrictions and so on	Vendor and purchaser

Home Construction: From Foundation to Finish

Sometimes, the prospective homeowner may opt to build his/her dream home instead of buying a house that has already been built. This option may result in a more customized effect for the homeowner on completion of the construction process. It is necessary to mention that the financing and construction processes under this arrangement can be more challenging. It is extremely important for you (the prospective homeowner) to know how you will finance the construction of your home. Most financial institutions can provide advice on the loan amount for which you can qualify based on your financial position.

Process for Building a Home

1. Use suitable land that you own or acquire land ensuring there are adequate utilities such as water and electricity and has the requisite Town and Country Planning approvals.
2. As in the purchase of a home a prequalification assessment must be done to determine the level of financing that can be obtained.
3. Enlist the services of an architect/draughtsman to prepare house plans.
4. Obtain approval from Town and Country Planning division.
5. Submit the approved plans and engineer's/surveyors' estimate the costs of raw materials to the financial institution and apply for a bridge financing facility.
6. Enter into a builder's contract.
7. Budget for additional costs.
8. Obtain a builder's estimate and quantity surveyor's report.
9. Ensure proper terms and conditions of the bridging facility are negotiated.
10. Begin construction.
11. Obtain completion certificate and inspection certificates from relevant authorities and replace bridging finance loan with the mortgage which is considerably cheaper.

Prequalification Assessment

As with the purchase of a home, if you decide to build your dream house and you require funds from a financial institution, it is advisable to obtain advice on the loan amount for which you are likely to qualify by doing a prequalification assessment.

After evaluating the information, the financial institution will determine the maximum loan amount for which the purchaser qualifies. The prequalification assessment is considered to be the initial step in the acquisition of a construction loan and it can lead to a relationship with the financial institution of your choice.

Construction Loans and Bridge Financing Facilities

A construction loan, referred to as bridge financing (offered by a financial institution), is provided during the construction period and replaced with a mortgage on the completion of the building—that is on receipt of the various completion approvals from government authorities. The amount approved for a construction loan is normally based on the cost of construction and the projected value of the property being constructed. The disbursement of funds is based on the progress of the construction work. Upon completion of construction, and once the relevant certificates and inspections are finalized, the construction loan is converted into a residential mortgage.

The key parties involved in the construction process include:

- Prospective homeowner—The owner of the land on which the house will be constructed
- The Financial institution—The Institution from which construction or bridging finance will be made available
- Builder—The person who will build the house from foundation to finish

- Architect/draughtsman—The individual who finalizes the design and produces house plans
- Quantity surveyor—The person who manages costs related to building of the house, from the initial calculations through to the project's final figures

Helpful Hint—Home Construction:

- ***Determine the amount of funds available.*** This is personal funds plus the amount approved under the prequalification assessment as this will determine the size and type of house.
- ***Develop a portfolio of preferred designs and photographs of properties you like.*** This will help the persons you are hiring to design and construct your home in keeping with your vision. Use the Internet and drive around areas that have the kinds of houses you are thinking of to get fresh ideas and design.
- ***Invite a surveyor, builder, and/or architect to do a site visit prior to agreeing on design and price.*** This will ensure that the proposed design of the building takes advantage of the location and all associated costs for land preparation are included in the total cost.
- ***Shop around before choosing a contractor or builder.*** View the previous work of a few contractors from references. Ensure that the contractor has a good reputation for delivering in a timely manner and within budget. This is a very important step that should not be dismissed as it can save you a lot of problems when the house is being built.
- ***Keep the square footage, finishing touches, and interior simple.*** Any changes in design or area can result in an escalation of cost and may need plans to be resubmitted for approval. This takes time and money.

It is important that you know all the cost and fees involved in home construction so that you can budget for them. There are a number of documents that the financial institution will require to process a construction loan as follows:

Quantity surveyor's report—This document outlines the cost of construction given market conditions and valuation as determined by a qualified quantity surveyor and is also required at different stages in the building process on application for disbursement of funds from the lender.

Insurance premiums—Contractors' all-risk insurance must be taken out during the period of the construction. This is also a requirement of most financial institutions. Upon completion of construction, homeowner's comprehensive insurance must be taken out to cover the replacement cost of the building.

Personal Information

- Evidence of nationality (identification card, driver's permit, or Passport)
- Evidence of income (job letter and pay slip)
- Statements of loans
- Statements of savings
- Evidence of current address (copy of utility bill).

Property Information

- Title deed or lease
- This is a legal document to prove your ownership of the land on which the house is being constructed.

Survey Plan

- This document has drawings of the land, its boundaries, and physical objects on the land. This plan is prepared and signed by a licensed surveyor.

Property (Land) Tax Receipts

- These receipts confirm that the tax payments on the property are up to date and there are no pending claims by the relevant authority.

Lease Rent Receipt (Applicable Where Land Is Leasehold)

- This is a receipt from the lessor (e.g., a regional authority or an individual), confirming that the lease payments are up to date.

Town and Country Planning Approval

- House plans must be approved by the Town and Country Planning Division prior to starting construction.
- Regional Corporation Approval is also required.
- House plans must also be approved by the Local Regional Authority prior to construction.

Builders' Estimate

- This is an estimate of the cost to build the house from "foundation to finish," prepared by the person contracted to do the job. It includes labor and material costs. References from the builder's previous clients are also required by mortgage lenders.

Quantity Surveyor's Report

- This is an estimate of the final construction cost of the building based on current market conditions. The report must be prepared by a licensed quantity surveyor.

Projected Valuation Report (Post Construction)

- This is a report which details the estimated value of the property on completion of the construction according to the specifications of the drawings.

Deed of Mortgage

- When the loan is approved by the financial institution, the borrower will be required to transfer or convey his/her right to the ownership of a property to the lender (financial institution) through a deed of mortgage as security for the loan on completion of the construction process.

Upon Completion of Construction

The following approvals, clearances, and documents are required to obtain an amortized mortgage to replace the more expensive bridging finance:

Electrical Inspectorate Certificate—The certificate is issued by the Government Electrical Inspectorate and confirms that the wiring and electrical installation in the building are in accordance with its regulations.
Re-inspection Valuation—This is a post-construction confirmation that the final value of the property is not less than the original estimates.
Water and Sewage Authority Clearance Certificate—This certifies approval of the water and wastewater plumbing designs by the relevant authority.
Completion Certificate—This document confirms that the house or building has been successfully constructed in accordance with approved plans. The certificate is issued by the office of the Local Regional Authority.

Finalization of Mortgage Contract

When building a home, the finalization of the mortgage contract is tedious and time-consuming. While the process is similar to buying property, the following differences should be noted in terms of the process required to finalize the construction loan and convert it into a mortgage contract:

(i) Loan funds are disbursed on a phased basis *(drawdowns)*, made based on the progress of the project and must be supported by measurement and valuation provided by the quantity surveyor.
(ii) Interest is payable on the accumulated sums drawn down only and not the total loan approved.
(iii) Interest payment begins with the disbursement of the first drawdown and continues until the issuance of a completion certificate on the property. This is called bridging interest.

(iv) On completion of construction a completion certificate must be obtained from the relevant regional corporation.
(v) An up-to-date valuation report must NOW be requested from the valuator. When all the clearances, approvals, and documents listed above are obtained, the lender converts the bridging loan into an amortized mortgage loan and the homeowner and mortgagor commence to pay both principal and interest.

When building a home you will be required to enter into a builder's contract. A builder's contract is an agreement entered into by the builder/contractor who will build the house and the client.

A builder's contract will contain inter alia:

- The agreed price at which the project will be done. It is very common to have an escalation clause that will cover any increases in the cost of material and/or labor and the reason why changes should not be made after signing of contract where possible. This increase will be for the account of the client.
- The scope of works that will be done by the builder/contractor
- A list of the materials and specification of the materials that the builder/contractor will provide
- The mobilization fee that will be needed
- The time frame in which the project will be completed
- Any penalty for not completing within the specified time
- The value of any materials to be supplied by the client
- Guarantee of the works within a specified time period
- The completion certificate, which will include electrical and plumbing certification

If there is a cost overrun on construction, additional funding will have to be renegotiated with the financial institution. However if the individual is at the ceiling or maximum amount that he/she qualifies for, financing the cost overruns can be problematic. When you construct your own home you can create greater value than when purchasing a home.

Other Considerations for Home Ownership

The term "home equity" refers to the money value of your home in excess of any outstanding debts such as mortgages or liabilities. For example, if you have a house for which the current fair market value is $500,000 (this should be based on an official appraisal) and a mortgage balance of $350,000, then you have $150,000 of home equity. Every month as you make your mortgage contribution, you repay part of the capital; you increase your home equity as the loan payment includes interest and capital repayment. Many mortgages allow earlier capital payments and can result in the reduction in the life of the mortgage and increase your equity. Similarly when you do capital improvements it increases your equity.

There are a number of effective ways to pay your mortgage off in a shorter period of time in order to build equity in your home. You can make a higher initial down payment or make extra principal payments. However the mortgage contract must contain clauses for balloon payment without penalty. Equity in your home can be utilized in several ways. The primary manner in which it can be used is in securing a home equity loan or a second mortgage to facilitate inter alia:

- Covering expenses of major emergencies, for example a huge medical bill (if you do not have sufficient savings or inadequate medical insurance)
- Financing education
- Engaging in crucial home improvements projects and renovations
- Consolidating your various debts into one monthly payment.

Types of Insurance Relative to Homeownership (See Chap. 6)

With regard to home ownership, one type of insurance that home owners are encouraged to purchase is homeowner's insurance. This type of insurance allows the owner of the property to receive compensation in the event of any loss or damage as long as the policy's annual premium payments are kept up to date. Another type of insurance is the **Mortgage Installment Protection Plan**. This policy has several benefits:

- Pays your mortgage and related expenses if you become temporarily disabled due to an accident or sickness which results in a loss of income.
- Pays the outstanding balance if you become permanently or totally disabled.
- Waives your premium for a specific period if you become unemployed.
- Waives your premium for a specific period if there is foreclosure on your property.

This type of insurance is characterized by a premium being paid only once to the insurer at the time of disbursement of the mortgage loan and forms part of the closing costs associated with a mortgage transaction. Generally, the mortgage lender will have a group policy covering its mortgage holders where the premiums are lower than the individual insurance rate.

The purpose of this type of insurance is to provide additional "protection" to the financial institution in the event that the borrower defaults in his/her payments under certain specific circumstances.

Additional Considerations for Property Value Coverage

In addition to the insurance coverage mentioned above, you can make enquires at your financial institution or insurance provider for information on the following insurance options for property value coverage:

- Replacement value (recommended)—When applying for the comprehensive homeowner's insurance cover, clients should ensure that they are covered for the replacement value (the cost to rebuild the building "as is").
- Cover mortgage debt—Insuring the property to cover the value of the debt only leaving the homeowner exposed in the event of damage to the property.

- Inclusion of out-of-pocket expenses—When selecting insurance coverage, one should also consider the other expenses that are likely to be incurred in the event of damage to property, including
    - Rental of alternate premises while the property is under construction;
    - Demolition of the existing structure (where applicable); and
    - Removal of rubble from site.
- Individual or group plans provided by mortgagee—Some mortgage lenders have developed group plans that cover all risks associated with the property, and this is generally more cost-effective than providing an individual policy to cover the risks.
- Insurance will not cover all the costs of restoring the insured property but it will go a long way toward helping the cause. The mortgagee normally dictates the insurance coverage which must at least be equal to the loan granted. The insured will also need to decide how much risk he/she is prepared to assume. There is risk involved when the insurance coverage for property is less than 100% of the replacement value (underinsured). This would actually work against the insured as the average clause of the policy will apply. The formula used for determining the ***amount of settlement*** is as follows:

$$(\text{Sum insured} / \text{Replacement value}) \times \text{Amount of loss} = \text{Amount of Settlement.}$$

- If you decide that you are only going to insure your property at 50% of its replacement value, the insurance company will take for granted that you have assumed 50% of the risk and will pay you only 50% of the amount of the loss suffered in the event of a claim.
- For example, if the replacement value of your property is $100,000.00, and you decide to insure it for 50% of the value or $50,000.00. If the property is totally destroyed, the insurance company will pay you only the sum insured of $50,000, calculated as follows:

$$(\text{Sum insured} / \text{Replacement value}) \times \text{Amount of loss} = \text{Amount of Settlement}$$

$$\text{Substituting values}: (\$50{,}000 / \$100{,}000) \times \$100{,}000 = \$50{,}000$$

- This is 50% of the replacement cost or loss suffered. Although you can expect to get the full sum insured of $50,000 because you suffered a total loss, you will still have to find the other 50% or $50,000 to restore the property. Let us take the example of a partial loss. Assuming you had only a partial loss that would cost you $80,000 to restore your home you can expect to receive only:

$$\text{Substituting values}: (\$50{,}000 / \$100{,}000) \times \$80{,}000 = \$40{,}000$$

- This is 50% of the loss suffered. You will have to finance the other $40,000 to restore your property. However, if you had insured your home at the full replacement value or $100,000, you would have received the full amount of the loss suffered.
- By the same token, one should not overinsure your property as you would not be entitled to more than the replacement cost of your property. It is therefore very important that you pay close attention to the replacement cost of your property when the policy is renewed and ensure that the sum insured is close to the replacement cost. If it is not, you will have to pay the shortfall. It is therefore imperative that your insurance coverage always reflects the updated valuation of your property. Using one broker or agent for all your insurance can result in substantial discounts.
- Certain physical improvements such as fire extinguishers on your property, or smoke detectors or deadbolts on all external doors would be considered in obtaining discounts in insurance premiums. One can reduce your home insurance risk by taking the time to invest in a few relatively inexpensive safety devices and reduce the likelihood of an unfortunate event occurring. Examples of safety devices include:

  - Adequate burglar-proofing,
  - Smoke detectors in your house,
  - Easily accessible and functional fire extinguishers in your house, and
  - Home security systems.

Special discounts apply to individuals over 50 years or 60 years who have membership in retirement organizations.

Renting Option

Buying or building is usually the best long-term investment, but you can consider renting if:

- You do not have the funds and cannot obtain a loan to build or buy your home
- You do not have the down payment needed in order to qualify for a loan
- Your rent is very low and you are saving to build or buy a home.

The process for renting a home is as follows:

1. Work out your budget
2. Start your search for an apartment, townhouse, or house to rent
3. Successful viewings
4. Reserving the property
5. Process your application
6. Agree to your tenancy
7. Prepare to move in
8. Move in

Rental Agreements

A lease or rental agreement is a contract. It forms the legal basis for your relationship with your landlord by setting out important issues such as:

- The length of your tenancy,
- The amount of rent and deposit(s) you are required to pay,
- The number of people who can live in the rental property,
- Who pays for utilities,
- Whether you may have pets,
- Whether you may sublet the property,
- The landlord's access to the rental property, and
- Whose job it is to maintain and repair the premises.

It is important that a lease or rental agreement is in writing and both the landlord and tenant sign as agreeing with the terms and conditions of the contract. The rights and responsibilities of both parties are spelled out and can be used as a source of reference for the settlement of disputes that may arise between the two parties. It is important that you have an attorney vet the lease prior to commitment. The tenant should examine the following before entering into a rental agreement:

1. The physical condition of the rental property,
2. Level of security,
3. Health, safety, and sanitary conditions,
4. Availability of electricity, water, and sewer services, and
5. Deliverables stated in the agreement are in working condition.

Termination of Rental Agreement

A rental agreement is valid for the term specified in the agreement. The landlord or tenant may choose to give prior notice of intention to renew or not renew the agreement or may be terminated before the term specified where there is a breach of the terms and conditions by either party.

Rent-to-Own

The biggest argument against renting is that rent payments do not contribute to your purchase of the asset, unless special arrangements are made to achieve this, for example, the Rent-to-Own option as offered by the Housing Development Corporation (HDC). This program was developed as an initiative to target the lower-income segment of society for persons who are unable to service a mortgage. It can be seen as an attempt to bridge the gap between renting and owning property. Further information on this initiative is available on the website of the Housing Development Corporation.

Options, Issues, Pros, and Cons of Renting

When you are renting you are required to pay:

- An initial security deposit (normally refundable),
- Monthly rental,
- Utility bills, and
- Contents insurance (optional but advisable).

The pros of renting a home include:

- Shelter that is affordable and readily available even though you cannot afford to own a home,
- Structural maintenance of the premises is normally borne by the landlord, and
- Ease of relocating when the rental agreement expires.

The cons of renting a home include:

- Rent is consumption spending for shelter as you do not build equity in the property.
- The landlord may opt to increase your rent at the end of your agreement.
- Increases in rental rates are normally larger than increases in your income.
- On retirement your income normally decreases, but rental rates tend to continue increasing.
- There is no security of tenure. When your rental agreement expires, it may not be renewed by the landlord.

You may have to accept several restrictions, for example:

- Limited ability to personalize space (structural changes)
- Pets may be prohibited.
- Limits on entertaining, such as parties.
- Children may not be allowed.
- Accommodation may be limited to singles, married couples, and so on.

8

Introduction to Entrepreneurship

The word "entrepreneur" derives from the French words *entre*, meaning "between," and *prendre*, meaning "to take." The word was originally used to describe people who "take on the risk" or who "undertake" a task, such as starting a new venture. Inventors and entrepreneurs differ from one another; an inventor creates something new whereas an entrepreneur assembles and then integrates all the resources needed to transform the invention into a viable business. Entrepreneurship (according to the classic definition) is the process by which individuals pursue opportunities without regard to resources they currently control.

Why Become an Entrepreneur?

The three primary reasons that people become entrepreneurs and start their own firms are as follows:

(a) Be **your own boss**. Many entrepreneurs want to be their own boss because they have a long-term ambition to own their own business or they have become frustrated working in traditional jobs.

C. Sahadeo, *Financial Literacy and Money Script*,
https://doi.org/10.1007/978-3-319-77075-8_8

(b) Pursue **their own ideas**. Some people recognize ideas for new products or services and they have a desire to see those ideas realized.
(c) Realize **financial goals.** People start their own firms to pursue financial rewards. This motivation, however, is typically secondary to the first two and often fails to live up to its hype.

Characteristics of Successful Entrepreneurs

1. *Passion for the Business*
   The number one characteristic shared by successful entrepreneurs is passion for their business. This passion typically stems from the entrepreneur's belief that the business will positively influence people's lives.
2. *Product/Customer Focus*
   A successful entrepreneur has a keen focus on products and customer service. This typically stems from the fact that most successful entrepreneurs are extroverted.
3. *Tenacity Despite Failure*
   Entrepreneurs have a higher threshold for failure. Even with research and careful planning, entrepreneurs venture into new waters and are inevitably faced with much risk. Developing a new business always require a certain degree of experimentation to improve or modify an existing product or service or develop a new proposition altogether. Setbacks and failures inevitably occur during this process. The litmus test for entrepreneurs is their ability to persevere through setbacks and failures.
4. *Execution Intelligence*
   The ability to fashion a solid business idea into a viable business is a key characteristic of successful entrepreneurs. The ability to effectively execute a business idea means developing a business model, putting together a new venture team, raising money, establishing a partnership, managing finances, leading and motivating employees, and so on. It also demands the ability to translate thought, creativity, and imagination into action and measurable results.

Common Myths About Entrepreneurs

Myth 1: Entrepreneurs are born, not made.

This myth is based on the mistaken belief that some people are genetically predisposed to becoming an entrepreneur. Sometimes entrepreneurs are characterized as extroverts, but this is not necessarily true. Many enrepreneurs are "temporary dreamers" but they are agile and quick to respond to opportunity.

Myth 2: Entrepreneurs are gamblers.

Entrepreneurs are moderate to huge risk-takers, as are most people; but they take calculated risks and cannot be classified as gamblers.

Myth 3: Entrepreneurs are motivated primarily by money.

Albeit entrepreneurs may be motivated by financial rewards, this is not the primary purpose of an entrepreneur as the excitement and adrenalin flow are the main motivation for many.

Myth 4: Entrepreneurs should be young and energetic.

Whereas entrepreneurs should have high energy levels, this does not exclude older persons. Investors often cite the strength of the entrepreneur (in terms of business experience, skill, and talent) as their most important criteria in the decision to fund a new venture. Many persons have become successful entrepreneurs on retirement!

Types of Start-Up Firms

Salary-substitute firms are small firms that afford their owner or owners a similar level of income to what they would earn in a conventional job. Examples of salary-substitute firms are dry cleaners, convenience stores, restaurants, accounting firms, retail stores, and hairstyling salons.

Lifestyle firms provide their owner or owners the opportunity to pursue a particular lifestyle and earn a living while doing so. Examples of lifestyle firms include gym instructors, golf pros, and tour guides.

Entrepreneurial firms bring new products and services to market by creating and seizing opportunities. Google and Facebook are well-known, highly successful examples of entrepreneurial firms.

Changing Demographics of Entrepreneurs

Women Entrepreneurs

1. There were 11.6 million women-owned businesses employing 9 million people and generating $1.7 trillion in sales as of 2017 in the United States.
2. The top industry for women-owned businesses is "Other servives including pet care institutions and beauty salons" (23 % of all women owned firms), "health care and social assistance" (15%) and "professional/scientific."
3. Women-owned firms still trail male-owned businesses in terms of sales and profits.

Minority Entrepreneurs

1. There has been a substantial increase in minority entrepreneurs in the USA from 1996 to 2010.
2. The biggest jump has come in Latino entrepreneurs, whose share increased from 11% to 23% from 1996 to 2010, followed by Asian entrepreneurs, whose share jumped from 4% to 6% during the same period.
3. While these numbers are encouraging, in general the firms created by minority entrepreneurs lag behind averages for all firms in terms of economic indicators. The Kauffman Foundation is one group that is actively engaged in research to not only track the growth of minority entrepreneurs but also better understand how to strengthen the infrastructure and networks to enable minority entrepreneurs to reach higher levels of financial success.

Senior Entrepreneurs

1. The increase in entrepreneurial activity among senior entrepreneurs, consisting of people 55 years and older, between 1996 and 2010 is substantial (from 14% to 23%).
2. This increase is attributed to a number of factors, including corporate downsizing, an increasing desire among older workers for more per-

sonal fulfillment in their lives, and growing worries among seniors that they need to earn additional income to pay for future healthcare services and other expenses.
3. There are a number of interesting statistics associated with the increasing incidence of senior entrepreneurs. For example, 39 is now the average age of the founders of technology companies in the USA, with twice as many over age 50 as under 25.

Young Entrepreneurs

1. Interestingly, a drop in new entrepreneurial activity for people in the 20–34 age range occurred between 1996 and 2010 (from 35% in 1996 to 26% in 2010); nonetheless, the number of young people interested in entrepreneurship remains strong.
2. At the high school and younger level, according to a Harris Interactive survey of 2438 individuals aged 8–21, 40% said they'd like to start their own business someday. On college campuses, interest in entrepreneurship education is at an all-time high. More than 2000 colleges and universities in the USA, which is about two-thirds of the total, offer at least one course in entrepreneurship.

Entrepreneurial Firms' Impact on Society

Entrepreneurial firms have a strong impact on the strength and stability of the economy and provides substantial job creation. With regard to innovation a 2010 Small Business Administration report stated that small firms (fewer than 500 employees) are providers of a significant share of innovations that take place in the USA. Small businesses are the creators of most new jobs in the USA and employ more than half of all private sector employees.

Given innovation is a critical component of entrepreneurship, these firms have a dramatic impact on society. Innovation results in new products and services that make our lives easier, enhance our productivity at work, improve our health, and entertain us. Many of these products and services were conceived and brought to market by entrepreneurial firms.

New innovations do create moral and ethical issues that societies are forced to grapple with. For example, bar-code scanner technology and the Internet have made it easier for companies to track the purchasing behavior of their customers, but this raises privacy concerns.

Entrepreneurial Firms' Impact on Larger Firms

In addition to the impact that entrepreneurial firms have on the economy and society, entrepreneurial firms have a positive impact on the effectiveness of larger firms. For example, some entrepreneurial firms are original equipment manufacturers, producing parts that go into products that larger firms manufacture and sell. They facilitate the process of outsourcing for larger firms. Many exciting new products, such as smartphones, digital cameras, and improved prescription drugs, are not solely the result of the efforts of larger companies with strong brand names. They were produced with the cutting-edge component parts or research and development efforts provided by entrepreneurial firms. The evidence shows that many entrepreneurial firms have built their entire business models around producing products and services that help larger firms be more efficient or effective or rather they partner with larger firms in win-win arrangements.

The Entrepreneurial Process

A. ***Decision to Become an Entrepreneur***

Often, a triggering event prompts an individual to become an entrepreneur. For example, an individual may lose his job or accept voluntary retirement and decide that the time is right to start her own business or even may have no choice but to start a business to feed oneself and family.

B. ***Developing Successful Business Ideas***

Successful businesses must have feasible business ideas. Developing a successful business idea includes opportunity recognition, feasibility analysis, writing down a business plan, industry and competitor analysis, and the development of an effective business model.

C. ***Moving from an Idea to an Entrepreneurial Firm***

The first step in becoming an entrepreneur is to research the many ideas that emerge and select the most feasible or viable option. Whereas failure will occur even with the best planning and execution, it is costly and proper planning and execution is critical for success. During the planning stage there must be preparation of the proper ethical and legal foundation, assess the viability of the new venture, build a new venture team, and prepare a projected income statement, start up capital requirements and a cash flow statement. The source of funding whether loan, equity, or savings should be determined early so arrangements can be put in place to fund the new venture.

D. ***Managing and Growing an Entrepreneurial Firm***

In today's competitive environment, all firms must ensure they understand the life cycle of a business and prepare and plan accordingly. The growth stage requires a thorough understanding of the market and industry. At this stage focus is on growth strategies, partnering with complementary offerings, strong marketing programs, confronting new ventures, and preparing and evaluating the challenges of growth.

Creativity, Innovation, and Entrepreneurship

One of the tenets of entrepreneurship is the ability to create new and useful products and services that solve the problems and challenges that people face every day. Entrepreneurs can create value in a number of ways. The success of Amazon is just one example of technology and vision. What about Mark Zuckerberg, an American technology entrepreneur best known for co-founding facebook. The roles entrepreneurs play include the introduction of new products and services, development of new technology, discovery of knowledge, improvement of existing products or services, and finding innovative ways of providing more valuable goods and services with fewer resources.

Creativity is the ability to develop new ideas and discover new ways of looking at problems and opportunities. Creativity is essential to survival. Creativity is an important source for building a competitive advantage. Entrepreneurs must develop new insights into the relationship among resources, needs, and values. A ***paradigm*** is a preconceived idea of what the world is, what it should be like, and how it should operate. These ideas become so deeply rooted in our minds that they become blocks to creative thinking, even though they may be outdated, obsolete, and no longer relevant. Paradigms stifle creativity when they limit or restrict the way people think about possible solutions. Paradigms set parameters and cause thinking to be based on past "rules and procedures" rather than open, creative thinking that can lead to innovative solutions. Creative and innovative thought must break through the barriers that paradigms present.

The question is whether creativity can be taught? Research shows that anyone can learn to be creative. Research into the working of the human brain shows that each hemisphere of the brain processes information differently. One side of the brain tends to be dominant over the other. The human brain develops asymmetrically, and each hemisphere tends to specialize in certain functions. The left brain handles language, logic, and symbols. The right brain takes care of the body's emotional, intuitive, and spatial functions. Therefore steps in enhancing creativity include becoming an expert, generating ideas, be open and aware and even playing and pretending. Creativity is the act of coceiving or developing an original idea.

Innovation is the ability to apply creative solutions to problems and opportunities. Innovation must be a constant process because even successful businesses need to innovate to remain viable. Innovation and creativity work in tandem.

Entrepreneurship is the result of a disciplined, systematic process of applying creativity and innovation to ideas, needs, and opportunities in the marketplace. Entrepreneurs learn to tap their innate creativity by breaking down the barriers to creativity that most of us have. Entrepreneurship requires both left- and right-brained thinking.

Barriers to Creativity

There are many barriers to creativity—time pressures, unsupportive management, pessimistic coworkers, overly rigid company policies, and countless others. The most difficult hurdles are sometimes those we impose on ourselves. Ten "mental blocks" that limit individual creativity include:

1. Searching for just one right answer
2. Focusing on being logical
3. Blindly following rules
4. Constantly being practical
5. Viewing play as frivolous
6. Becoming overly specialized
7. Avoiding ambiguity
8. Fearing looking foolish
9. Fearing mistakes and failure
10. Believing that "I'm not creative"

Questions to spur the imagination include:

1. Is there a new way to do it?
2. Can you borrow or adapt it?
3. Can you give it a new twist?
4. Do you merely need more of the same?
5. Do you need less of the same?
6. Is there a substitute?
7. Can you rearrange the parts?
8. What if you do just the opposite?
9. Can you combine ideas?
10. Are customers using your product or service in ways you never expected or intended?
11. Which customers are you not servicing? What changes to your product or service are necessary to reach them?
12. Can you put it to other uses?
13. What else could we make from this?
14. Are there other markets for it?
15. Can you reverse it?
16. Can you rearrange it?
17. Can you put it to another use?
18. What idea seems impossible, but if executed, would revolutionize your business?

How to Enhance Creativity

The right environment can encourage people to develop and cultivate ideas. It is important that workers have the freedom and the incentives to be creative and are rewarded and recognized for their creativity.

Entrepreneurs can stimulate their own creativity and encourage it among workers by:

1. Including creativity as a core company value;
2. Hiring for creativity;
3. Establishing an organizational structure that nourishes creativity;
4. Embracing and rewarding diversity;
5. Expecting creativity and also tolerating failure;
6. Incorporating fun into the work environment—encouraging curiosity;
7. Designing a work space that encourages creativity;
8. Viewing problems as challenges;
9. Providing creativity training and support;
10. Developing a procedure for capturing ideas;
11. Talking and interacting with customers;
12. Monitoring emerging trends and identifying ways your company can capitalize on them—anticipate what the customer wants; remember Steve Jobs said, "Tell the customer what he wants."

Individuals can be creative using the following techniques:

1. Forget the "rules."
2. Give your mind fresh input every day—travel and observe. Spend time with nature.
3. Observe the products and services of other companies, especially those in completely different markets.
4. Recognize the creative power and opportunities that mistakes can offer.
5. Keep a journal handy to record your thoughts and ideas.
6. Listen to other people, including customers.
7. Watch a movie.
8. Talk to a child.
9. Do something ordinary in an unusual way.

10. Keep a toy box in your office.
11. Do not throw away seemingly "bad" ideas.
12. Read books on stimulating creativity or take a class on creativity.
13. Take some time off. Take quiet time. Take time for introspection on a daily basis.
14. Be persistent.

The Creative Process

Although new ideas may appear to strike like a bolt of lightning, they are actually the result of the creative process. The creative process involves seven steps:

1. Preparation
2. Investigation
3. Transformation
4. Incubation
5. Illumination
6. Verification
7. Implementation

Techniques for Improving the Creative Process

Brainstorming is a process in which a small group or team interacts with only basic rules of respect but otherwise with wide liberties and very little structure to produce a large number of novel and imaginative ideas. For a successful brainstorming session an entrepreneur should practice the following guidelines:

1. Keep the group small—five to eight members and make the group as diverse as possible.
2. Start the session with some form of exercise, preferably aerobic exercise.
3. At the onset outline the rule that "company rank and department affiliation are irrelevant."

4. Give the group a well-defined problem to address and provide the relevant background information about the problem in advance.
5. Limit the session to 40–60 minutes.
6. Take a field trip to visit the scene of the problem.
7. Appoint someone for the job of recorder.
8. Use a seating pattern that encourages communication.
9. Throw logic out of the window and encourage all ideas from the team, even wild and extreme ones. Write down all ideas irrespective how outlandish it may seem.
10. Forbid evaluation or criticism.
11. Encourage "idea hitch-hiking."
12. Dare to imagine the unreasonable.

Mind mapping is an extension of brainstorming. Mind mapping is a graphical technique that encourages thinking with both sides of the brain, visually displays the various relationships between ideas, and improves the ability to view the problem from many sides. It relates to the way the brain actually works. Rather than throwing out ideas in a linear fashion, the brain jumps from one idea to another. In many creative sessions, ideas are rushing out so fast that many are lost if a person attempts to shove them into a linear outline.

The mind mapping process works differently and the following are some examples:

1. Sketch a picture to symbolize the problem.
2. Write down every idea that comes to your mind—use key words and symbols.
3. When idea flow starts to trickle, stop, take a rest. Restart when you are in the right frame of mind, when you are suffiently re-energized.

Focus Groups

A focus group is a gathering of 5–10 people who are selected because of their interest in a given issue being discussed. Although focus groups are used for a variety of purposes, they can be used to help generate new business ideas. The strength of focus groups is that they help companies uncover what's on their customers' minds through the give-and-take nature of a group discussion. The weakness is that because the participants do not always represent a random sample, the results may not be representative of larger groups.

Library and Internet Research

Libraries are often an underutilized source of information for generating business ideas. The best approach to utilizing a library is to discuss your general area of interest with a reference librarian, who can point out useful resources. Internet research is also important. Google or Bing will produce links to newspaper and magazine articles about the "hottest" and "latest" new business ideas. If you have a specific idea in mind, a useful technique is to set up a Google or Yahoo! "e-mail alert" using keywords that pertain to your topic of interest. Some other techniques include customer advisory boards that meet regularly to discuss needs, wants, and problems that may lead to new ideas. Libraries also provide good research material so that you do not have to start your project research from rock bottom.

Protecting Your Ideas

Entrepreneurs must understand how to get patents, copyrights, and trademarks to work for them. A ***patent*** is a government authority conferring a right or title, the sole right to make, use, or sell some invention to an individual or organization. Most patents are granted for new product inventions, but design patents, which extend beyond the date the patent is issued, are given to inventors who make new or original and ornamental changes in the designs of existing products that enhance their sales. A device cannot be patented if it has been in print anywhere in the world.

Information on patents in Trinidad and Tobago can be obtained from the following websites:

http://www.ttconnect.gov.tt/gortt/portal/ttconnect/Bus_investor Detail/?WCM_GLOBAL_CONTEXT=/gortt/wcm/connect/gortt+

web+content/TTConnect/Business/Role/AnInvestor/LawsandTaxes/Intellectual+Property+Rights
http://www.wipo.int/pct/guide/en/gdvol2/annexes/tt.pdf

A copy of the Patents Act is available at: http://rgd.legalaffairs.gov.tt/laws2/alphabetical_list/lawspdfs/82.76.pdf

A patent process generally involves the following six steps:

1. Establish the invention's novelty
2. Document the device
3. Search existing patents
4. Study search results
5. Submit the patent application
6. Prosecute the patent application

A ***trademark*** is any distinctive word, phrase, symbol, design, name, logo, slogan, or trade dress that a company uses to identify the origin of a product or to distinguish it from other goods in the market.

A ***service mark*** is the same as a trademark, except that it identifies and distinguishes the source of a service rather than a product.

A ***copyright*** is an exclusive right that protects the creators of original works of authorship such as literary, dramatic, musical, and artistic works. This includes motion pictures, software, choreography, books, and recordings.

Protecting intellectual property is imperative. Unfortunately, not every businessperson respects the rights of ownership to products, processes, names, and works. The dynamics of the global market makes protecting intellectual property even more challenging. The primary weapon is efficient use of the legal system. Before bringing a lawsuit, an entrepreneur must consider the following issues:

1. Can the opponent afford to pay if you win?
2. Will you get enough from the suit to cover the costs of hiring an attorney?
3. Can you afford the loss of time and privacy from the ensuing lawsuit?

Class Discussion

Want Help Fine-Tuning a Business Idea? Find a Coach/Mentor

1. If you were working on fine-tuning a business idea, would you check out a business chamber or an association that provides mentoring and advice for business founders? Why or why not?
2. To what degree do you believe that having a coach or mentor can make the difference between an entrepreneur succeeding or failing? In what areas of the entrepreneurial process do you believe that coaches and mentors are called upon the most?

Operational Management

Even in the smallest business a number of key tasks, or functions, must be done regularly. Stock must be bought, bills must be paid, customers must be served, and customer enquiries must be answered. In a small firm, all these jobs may be done by one or two people. In a large organization, people specialize in different tasks. Larger organizations for example have buyers to purchase the stock, accounts staff to pay the bills, checkout staff to serve customers, and customer service staff to answer queries.

Core Functional Areas of a Business

In a large organization, it is usually easier to identify separate functional areas because people work together in departments. Each department carries out the tasks that relate to its particular area. The main ones you are likely to meet in business are shown below (Fig. 8.1). However in stat up companies many of the functions may be undertaken by one person, but as the company grows it would become necessary to populate these functional areas with person with the requisite skills.

The Purposes of Functional Areas

The separation of business activities into functional areas is to ensure that all important business activities are carried out efficiently. This is essential if the business is to achieve its aims and objectives. It is also a process of

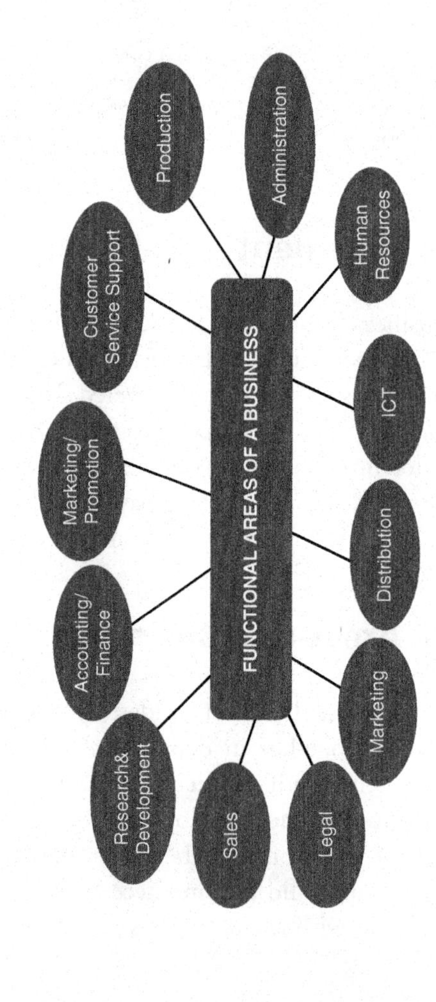

Fig. 8.1 Main functional areas of a business

assigning responsibilities for specific areas of the business. In addition, these functional areas will be responsible for supporting specific types of aims and objectives, for example:

- Sales and marketing will be involved in achieving targets linked to developing new markets or increasing sales.
- Human resources will be involved in arranging staff training activities and supporting the continuous professional development of all staff.
- Finance will be expected to monitor and support aims and objectives linked to keeping costs low to improve profitability.
- Production will be setting targets relating to quality or meeting the planned production schedules.

The Administration Function

Administration is a support function required by all businesses and includes a wide range of tasks, from preparing and monitoring budgets, routine administrative tasks include opening the mail, preparing and filing documents, and sending e-mails and faxes. Most administrators also deal with customer service and complaints. Poor or sloppy administration can be disastrous for a company's image and reputation. Efficient administration means that everything runs smoothly and managers can concentrate on the task of running the business. In a small organization, an administrator is often the "jack-of-all-trades."

The Customer Service Support Function

Customer service is critical to the success of any organization, big or small. Customer expectations are high. When people contact a business they expect a prompt, polite, and knowledgeable response. Technology demands an even faster response to customer complaints. Unless customers get a quality and efficient service they are likely to take their business elsewhere in the future. For this reason, many businesses have customer service staff—or a customer service department—where trained staff handle enquiries and complaints positively and professionally. As a matter of fact all staff in all organizations should be trained in customer service. Companies which are ISO quality certified must implement a system to recording all non conformances and taking corrective action which ensures improved customer service.

Organizations that manufacture and sell complex industrial products usually employ technical specialists or engineers in customer service to give detailed advice and information. Employees in customer service must have total knowledge of the products and services they offer. Similarly, computer suppliers like Dell or PC World, and Internet service providers like Telecommunication Services of Trinidad and Tobago (TSTT), have trained IT specialists to handle customer problems. Customer service staff also deal with complaints and problems. Most businesses have a special procedure for dealing with customer complaints to ensure these are dealt with quickly and consistently. Customer service staff must also be aware of the legal rights of customers—and this means having basic knowledge of consumer law.

The Distribution Function

Distribution means ensuring that goods are delivered to the right place, on time, and in the right condition. Some companies, such as Amazon, deliver direct to the customer, particularly when goods are bought online. Other businesses hold stocks in warehouses for delivery to stores around the area. Stores may use special vehicles for goods requiring special conditions and care such as chilled or frozen items. Other businesses which have to move more difficult loads or hazardous substances, such as large engineering parts, cars, or chemicals have to take special precautions as may be required by law.

Distribution involves more than just arranging for goods to be collected. For it to be cost-effective, costs must be kept as low as possible. In large countries working out the routes for many vehicles, with different loads—some urgent and some not—can be very complicated. Computer programs are used by staff skilled in logistics to work out the best routes. Many organizations outsource both storage and distribution to external contractors. This means paying a specialist firm to do the work. This may be cheaper than employing experts in the business.

The Accounting/Finance Function

Most entrepreneurs agree that this is the most important function in the business. Accounting staff record all the receipts and payments, sales and purchases so that cash flows are reported on a timely basis. Special journals are prepared for accruals and prepayments. The preparation of monthly or periodic management accounts and semi-annual and annual accounts must also be prepared from the accounting records which are maintained. This facilitates timely decisions based on accurate information. In some cases, this can mean the difference between the success and failure of the business as a whole.

The Human Resources (HR) Function

The human resources (HR) department covers all the employees of the organization. HR is responsible for recruiting new employees and ensuring that each vacancy is filled by the best person for the job. The recruitment process is expensive and time consuming. Hiring the wrong person can be costly. Firms should have orientation for new employees and should focus on continuous training and career development. Normally, new employees attend an **induction program or orientation** which tells them about the business, their rights and responsibilities as employees, the company rules, and the requirements of their new job. Arranging appropriate training and assisting with the continuous professional development of staff is another important aspect of HR. Training may be carried out in-house or externally.

An important function of HR is the retention of good, experienced, and specialized staff and therefore low turnover of staff. If turnover is too high it would result in disruption and higher training cost. However some turnover is necesary to ensure "new blood and ideas". While employees may leave for justifiable reasons, such as moving to another area or for promotion elsewhere, dissatisfaction with the job or the company, it is imperative that exit interviews are conducted. Employees normally have basic expectations of their employer. They expect to be treated and paid fairly, to have appropriate working conditions, and to have training opportunities supported by career advancement. These factors help **motivate staff and improves employee retention**. HR can help this process by monitoring working conditions, having staff welfare policies, and ensuring that company pay rates are fair and competitive.

The Legal Department Function

All organizations have to deal with legal matters which can be outsoured or death with inhouse. Changes in areas of e-commerce and globalization, as well as the increasing number of multinational organizations have brought about significant changes in the laws of many countries. Once a cost benefit anlaysis is done and the decision is taken to establish a legal department to oversee a firm's litigation and compliance with internal and external regulations and laws the firm must select persons with the necesary experience and expertise. Issues of corporate governance, intellectual property, legal administrative support, and litigation management, as well as mergers and acquisitions fall under the responsibility of this department. This department ensures that employees are kept up to date on workplace laws as well as customer complaints that cannot be handled by the Customer Support Services department.

The Information and Communication Technology (ICT) Function

Information and Communication Technology (ICT) is vital to any company's existence. Most crucial business tasks use computers or other technology-driven devices. The importance of data storage and retrieval is critical as any system failure can be catastrophic. Most organizations have a computer network where staff computers are linked through servers. Maintaining the servers and installing new (communal) software and additional hardware, such as printers and scanners, are part of the ICT function. ICT specialists generally are expected to update senior managers on technological developments. Above all, ICT is also used for system security. Making sure that only authorized users have access to the system, protecting the system against viruses and hackers, and ensuring there is a full back-up system to restore critical data in an emergency are vitally important.

The business website is likely to be technically maintained by the ICT staff, but the content will normally be devised by the marketing staff.

The Marketing/Promotion Function

Marketing is the management process responsible for identifying, anticipating, and satisfying customer requirements profitably. Marketing is an essential process to the success of the business. Marketing involves researching, packaging, and presenting products and services to consumers. Good marketing campaigns help grow sales and better inform consumers about the business. Another way to understand marketing is through the **marketing mix**, which consists of the four P's.

Product: Who are our customers? What do they want to buy and are their needs changing? Which products are we offering and how many are we selling? What new products are we planning?
In which areas are sales growing—and how can we sustain this?

Price: How much should we charge for the product or service? Can we charge different prices to different types of customers? What discounts can we give? What services or products should we give away or sell very cheaply and what benefits would this bring?

Promotion: How can we tell people about our products? Should we have specialist sales staff? Where should we advertise to attract the attention of our key customers? How else can we promote the product—should we give free samples or run a competition? Where and how can we obtain free publicity? Should we send direct mail shots and, if so, what information should we include?

Place: How can we distribute our product(s)? Should we sell directly to the customer or through retailers? Do we need specialist wholesalers or overseas agents to sell for us? The company needs to consider how social media can be used to market its products and services. Some of the questions we may ask are: What can we sell over the telephone? How can the Internet help us to sell more? Steve Jobs purports that one should start by identifying future customer needs. Products are then developed (or adapted) or services offered to meet these needs. If this is done well, it gives the company an edge over its competitors. This happened when Apple introduced the iPod. Marketing is responsible for the promotional activities which tell the customer what is available through advertising, sales promotions, and publicity campaigns. The company website is a major way of communicating with prospective and actual customers, and the style and content is usually the responsibility of marketing staff who ensure it is kept up to date. On line sales has been a successful measure introduced by many companies. They may also send regular newsletters to registered users of their site by e-mail. Monitoring the popularity of the website and obtaining information on the customers who use it may be undertaken by the company or outsourced to a specialist agency.

The Sales Function

Sales and after sales service are crucial functions for all businesses. It is pointless having superb products or services if no one buys them. For that reason, most businesses have sales targets as part of their aims and objectives. Meeting these is the responsibility of the sales staff or sales team. The job of the sales staff varies, depending upon the industry. Shops that sell basic products, such as chocolates or magazines, do not need to do much selling but more advertising and branding. For simple products and services, customers, choose the goods they want, pay, and leave. Customers expect more help and advice when buying a complex or expensive item, such as a television or car. Stores which sell these types of products therefore need trained sales staff who are friendly, knowledgeable, and can describe and/or demonstrate their products and link these to the customer's specific needs.

Business buyers also expect a high-quality service and in-depth advice and information. They may want to buy highly complex and expensive industrial equipment and need to negotiate special finance arrangements—particularly if they are overseas buyers. Business buyers will also expect discounts for bulk purchases. Sales representatives often travel to meet potential customers, as well as routinely visiting existing customers to ensure their needs are being met.

Employing a skilled sales force is expensive, especially if they are paid bonuses or commission. However, there are many benefits as an effective sales visit can convert enquiries into firm sales and build strong links with customers to encourage repeat business. There are strong links between marketing and sales—and in many businesses this may be a "joint" department. Sales can pass on important customer feedback to help marketing colleagues.

The Production Function

Production refers to the manufacture or assembly of goods. Production staff must ensure that goods are produced on time and are of the right quality. Quality requirements can vary considerably. While an error of 0.5 mm would not matter much for a chair or table, for an iPod or DVD player it would be critical. Checking quality does not mean just examining goods after they have been produced. Today quality control is "built-in" at every stage of the process, starting with the raw materials. Many buyers set down a detailed specification for the goods they order. For clothing, this includes the type and weight of material and the thread and fastenings too.

Production requires the use of input materials which must be purchased and which are used to produce new goods. The production is usually separated from purchasing and wharehousing. Buying raw materials is done by specialist purchasing staff, who take out contracts with regular suppliers and make sure that the terms of the contract are met, in relation to timely delivery, cost, quantity, and quality. The wharehouse staff ensure that all items are checked on delivery and refer any problems back to the supplier. The materials must be purchased at a competitive price to ensure the price of the final good is competitive.

If a manufacturer uses a large number of parts, such as a car maker, storage can be very expensive, in terms of the space required and the manpower to oversee the stock. For this reason, many manufacturers today operate a just-in-time (JIT) system. This involves having an agreement with specific suppliers to provide small quantities, quickly, when they are needed. This benefits both parties. The suppliers know that they have a regular buyer. The manufacturer no longer needs to store large quantities of goods or worry about not having sufficient stocks on the premises all the time. WallMart although not a manufacturer has one of the most effiicent JIT imventory system.

Production processes are automated. This means that machines or robots do all the routine or dangerous jobs. At a bottling plant, for example, the cleaning, filling, and labeling of the bottles is all done as a continuous process by machines. Operators check that the production "line" is functioning correctly by checking consoles and computer screens, as well as by watching the work as it progresses. Some industries use Computer Integrated Manufacturing, where the process is controlled by a computer.

When a process cannot be automated, teams of operators may work together and take responsibility for a sequence of operations. This makes the job more interesting and makes it easier to ensure high quality. This system is also more flexible because changes can easily be introduced at any stage by giving instructions to specific teams. It is therefore used by many car manufacturers who often want to vary certain models.

The production function also includes all the following aspects of production:

(i) **Production planning** involves close coordination with sales and marketing to ensure the production is timely and in keeping with customers' wants and needs. A realistic timescale must be predicted, bearing in mind other jobs that are in progress.

(ii) **Production control** means constantly checking progress to make sure that production plans are met—and taking remedial action if problems occur. This could be because of machinery breakdown, substandard raw materials, or labor shortages.

(iii) **Machine utilization control** is concerned with optimal use of equipment and minimizing problems by keeping all the equipment and machinery in good working order. This involves equipment being routinely checked and maintained. This is important because if a machine malfunctions it may produce damaged goods. If it breaks down completely, then production will cease. Because this aspect is so important, many organizations have a preventative maintenance plan, which shows the dates on which machines will be out of operation for inspection and servicing. These dates are then taken into consideration when production plans are made.

(iv) **Staff utilization** ensures that jobs are effectively co-ordinated and all the staff are working effectively and efficiently and concentrating their efforts on key production areas and targets. This is very important in industries which are labor-intensive and use more people than machines, such as assembling circuit boards or sewing uniforms.

(v) **Final quality checks** make certain that the product is of the correct standard. This can be done in several ways. Each item may be examined by hand or passed through a machine which checks that the size and tolerance are correct. Quality checks are also important for certain types of products. Alternatively, items may be selected for inspection on a random sampling basis. This would be the case if a large number of identical items are being produced, such as cups.

Research and Development (R & D) Function

This function is concerned with substantial improvements to existing products or product lines and new product development. In many industries, it also involves product design.

Improvements to existing products are often ongoing as a result of market research and development and customer feedback. Examples include microwavable containers and memory sticks for computers, mobile phones, Wi-Fi, and satellite navigation systems. New products may be developed because of scientific or technological scientific advances, or just a good idea such as Google or the Apple iPad. Research can be divided into two types. **Pure research** aims to help us to learn and understand more about anything and is usually carried out by universities and scientific establishments. **Applied research** is a focused investigation and intervention into how new discoveries are used to improve products and is usually done in business organizations (Table 8.1).

Table 8.1 Examples of links among the functional areas

Functional area	Links
Sales and production	Sales and production interact with each other to ensure customer orders are met without delay
Sales and accounting/finance	These two departments interact to ensure customers are screened before being allowed credit purchases or discounts; communication is also present when there are issues with customer payments
Distribution and accounting / finance	Invoices must accompany the sale and delivery of items
Sales and marketing/ promotion	Communication must take place to ensure the sales staff are aware and informed of any promotional activity being undertaken
Research and development and production	New product lines or methods of production are tested and perfected to increase efficiency and introduce new products
Human resource and accounting/finance	Agreements regarding salaries, wages, and bonuses are communicated and budgets agreed for training
Customer service support and research and development	Information pertaining to customer complaints, queries, advice, and specification of wants are relayed between departments to create new products or improve existing ones

Class Work

Safety Products makes airbags for cars. It aims to expand its operations over the next three years. It has the following departments: Sales, Production, Accounting/Finance, Distribution Marketing/Promotion, Research and Development, Human Resource, Customer Service, Marketing, and ICT.

For each target listed below, identify the functional area which would be mainly responsible for its achievement:

- increase output by 15%
- reduce outstanding debt levels
- employ 20 new production operatives
- develop "intelligent" airbags which adjust for individual occupants
- redesign the company website to be more appealing with extra features
- increase sales by 20%

Table 8.2 Procedure (including legal) for setting up a business in Trinidad and Tobago

No.	Procedures	Time to complete	Associated costs
1	Request company name To reserve a company name, the promoter must submit to the Companies Registry the statutorily prescribed Form 25. It is recommended that two alternative proposed names be submitted. After four days, the promoter must return to the Registry to collect the approved (stamped) form. All name approvals expire within three months	Four days	TTD 25
2	Statutory declaration before Commissioner of Affidavits Either an attorney-at-law or a person named in the incorporation documents as a director or secretary (if an attorney is not engaged in the company formation) must swear to a declaration of compliance (Form 31), which is a statutory declaration, before a duly certified Commissioner of Affidavits	One day	TTD 20
3	Registration with the Commercial Registry The properly completed documents are filed in person with the Commercial Registry, along with payment of the required fee. The company comes into existence, is legally registered, and acquires its own legal personality on the day on the date shown on its Certificate of Incorporation. However, it takes about four business days to obtain the Certificate of Incorporation, which provides required evidence for the company to undertake other procedures (e.g., registering with tax authorities). The following documents must be filed in duplicate: (a) Form 25, the company name request application; (b) Form 1, the embossed Articles of Incorporation; (c) Form 31, statutory declaration of compliance; (d) Form 4, notice of address of registered office; (e) Form 8, notice of directors; and (f) Form 27, notice of secretary. All forms are available at the government Printery	Four days	TTD 600 (TT$ 400 for Form 1; TT$ 40 for Form 31; TT$ 40 for Form 4; TT$ 40 for Form 8; TT$ 40 for Form 27; TT$ 40 for certificate of incorporation)
4[a]	Make a company seal The TTD 115 quoted is for a rubber company seal. A metal seal costs about TTD 400	Two days (simultaneous with the previous procedure)	TTD 115
5	Apply for tax payer identification number To apply for a taxpayer identification number, the company applies with the Board of Inland Revenue for a corporate file number and a pay-as-you-earn file number	One day	No charge

(*continued*)

Table 8.2 (continued)

No.	Procedures	Time to complete	Associated costs
6[a]	Apply for registration as an employer with National Insurance Board To obtain a national insurance number, the company must apply to register as an employer by completing an application form (NI.1) and filing it with the National Insurance Board of Trinidad and Tobago Employer registration is affected immediately upon receipt of the application except where the system data indicates previous registration of the employer. A Certificate of Registration is issued in the name of the company immediately following registration	One day (simultaneous with the previous procedure)	No charge
7[a]	Apply for registration of employees with the National Insurance Board After applying to be registered as an employer and receiving a national insurance number, the company must enroll with the National Insurance Board any qualifying employee who has not been enrolled previously. The employer must submit N1.4—the application to register an employed person with the National Insurance Board Service Centre within 14 days of hiring the employee. The employee is then required within seven days of employment, to provide the company with the information needed to complete Form NI.4. This form must be signed by the company and filed with the authority. It takes four weeks for the National Insurance Board Service Centre to notify the company that the application is in order and to supply the company with the employee's national insurance number	30 days (simultaneous with the previous procedure)	No charge
8[a]	Register for VAT If the company earns gross income over TTD 200,000 per year or if it anticipates earning such an income within 12 months from the date that it applies for VAT registration, it may apply by completing, signing, and filing two forms (VAT No. 1 and VAT No. 2) with the required supporting documentation. The company can start operating without being registered for VAT and apply only once it has reached the TTD 200,000 threshold. Upon registration, it will receive a certificate and a VAT registration number	30 days (simultaneous with the previous procedure)	No charge

Legal Requirements in Trinidad and Tobago: http://www.ttconnect.gov.tt/
[a]Takes place simultaneously with another procedure

Emotional Intelligence (EI or EQ): The Key to Success

Entrepreneurs and high-performance leaders need to combine high levels of technical expertise with superb people's skills—the ability to understand and motivate others commonly referred to as Emotional Intelligence (EI). The achievement of this competence begins with a strong level of individual awareness and understanding. Emotions are the captains of our lives, and we obey them without realizing it. EI is defined as a set of competencies that derive from a neural circuitry emanating in the limbic system. Thousands of studies have shown that effective leaders consistently possess more EI competencies such as self-awareness, self-management, social awareness, and relationship management.

Recent studies have shown that EI is a powerful key to effective leadership. In an ever-changing and dynamic business environment, organizational leaders must demonstrate more than technical and intellectual competence. Effective leaders must possess exemplary interpersonal skills in order to optimize team potential and performance. The core competencies of EI provide a platform to build and develop these skills.

Many businesses often view emotions as being too personal or unquantifiable to talk about in a meaningful way. However research has shown that all great leaders work through their emotions. Understanding the powerful role of emotions in the workplace sets the best leaders apart from the rest. In fact all the best leaders have not only found effective ways to understand and improve the way they handle their own personal emotions but the positive impact they have on the emotions of others. Quite simply, in any human group the leader has maximal power to sway everyone's emotions. When leaders drive emotions positively they bring the best in others. Scientists have referred to this process as the "open loop."

EI is important because it affects your ability to appreciate and understand other people's point of view and it allows you to anticipate how they are likely to respond. It therefore allows you to communicate with others in a pleasant, mature, and considerate way.

There is much empirical evidence on the importance and benefits of EI. The five dimensions of EI must be learnt, mastered, and practiced. These include the following:

- Self-Awareness (SA)
- Managing Emotion (ME)
- Motivation (M)
- Empathy (E)
- Social Skills (SS)

These are summarized as follows:

Self-awareness is explained as knowing yourself and what your emotions are telling you. This competence can be broken down into your ability to:

- Respect yourself
- Be positive
- Be true to yourself
- Give logic and rationality a rest
- Listen to others
- Understand your impact on others

Self-regulation is defined as being able to manage and control your own emotional state. This competence can be broken down into five key elements:

- Ability to defer judgment; curb impulse
- Ability to park the problem; detach yourself
- Ability to express yourself assertively rather than aggressively
- Ability to be flexible; go with the flow; don't force things
- Ability to manage your non-verbal communication

Motivation is explained as your ability to channel your emotions to enable you to achieve goals. Motivation can be subdivided into four key aspects:

- Striving to improve and to achieve high standards
- Being committed to achieving your goals
- Taking the initiative and seizing opportunities
- Being optimistic even in the face of adversity

Empathy deals with your ability to recognize and read emotions in others and is comprised of four key aspects:

- Being sensitive toward and understanding other people
- Making the needs and interests of others your point of reference
- Furthering the development of other people
- Being socially and politically tuned in

Social skill is defined as your ability to relate to and influence others and can be subdivided into three aspects:

- Developing and sustaining interpersonal relationships
- Communicating with others
- Working with others

In the workplace possessing cognitive intelligence is not sufficient. EI is important because it affects your ability to appreciate and understand other people's point of view and it allows you to anticipate how they are likely to respond and encourages all parties to work with each other in a pleasant, mature, and considerate way. In summary the following learning outcomes and practical skills required of a strong emotionally intelligent leader are as follows:

- Identification of the core competencies of EI
- Define and practice self-management, self-awareness, self-regulation, self-motivation, empathy, and social skills
- Leveraging EI to improve effectiveness as a leader
- Importance of perception
- Attitudes and behavior of leaders
- Remove emotional blind spot and integrate and apply EI to develop and transform personal and professional lives

9

Basic Financial Accounting

Accounting is the systematic process of identifying, recording, measuring, classifying, and communicating financial information. It applies a set of concepts, techniques, and rules so that financial information is reliable and comparable.

Users of Accounting Information

Individuals use accounting information although they may not apply the rigidity of accounting as for a business entity. Organizations set up accounting information systems to provide data for better decision-making. The information produced by the accounting process serves the needs of many users (or stakeholders) and in many instances it is mandatory as in the case of publicly listed companies. The different users of financial information can be classified as external and internal.

External users of accounting information are not directly involved in the day-to-day operations of the organization. External users are mostly concerned with the financial information which includes financial statements and narratives thereto which helps the stakeholder to analyze the organization's performance. *External users include:*

C. Sahadeo, *Financial Literacy and Money Script*,
https://doi.org/10.1007/978-3-319-77075-8_9

Bankers and Creditors—They loan money or other resources to the organization. Lenders need information that help them assess the organization's ability to repay its loan and debts. Lenders look at profit and loss account, balance sheet, and cash flow statement to determine the organization's ability to meet its debt obligations.

Shareholders (owners) of the business have legal control as they are entitled to attend and vote at its annual meetings. Shareholders bear the greatest risks, but in good times get all the excess rewards.

Prospective investors review and monitor the performance of the company by looking at the financial statements over a period of time and comparing them with other companies and the industry prior to making an investment decision.

External auditors' primary purpose is to enhance the degree of confidence of intended users in the financial statements and is a requirement for listed companies and other regulators. This is achieved by the expression of an opinion by the auditor on whether the financial statements are prepared, in all material respects, in accordance with an applicable financial reporting framework. Some financial analysts may use the accounting information to evaluate the financial health of the business for investment opportunities.

Employees and unions use the accounting information in assessing the company's performance and the fairness of their wages and future job prospects. The unions use the accounting information to negotiate terms and conditions of service for their members.

Regulators/government have legal authority or significant influence over the activities of organizations. They may need these reports to determine compliance, statistical data, and for taxation/regulatory purposes.

Internal users of accounting information are those directly involved in managing and operating the organization which includes *managers, officers, or other important internal decision-makers*. Internal users make the strategic and operating decisions for an organization. Management accounts are prepared on a monthly basis or more frequently if required. The role of accounting is to provide information to help improve the efficiency or effectiveness of an organization in delivering products or services.

Financial Versus Managerial Accounting

Financial accounting communicates the results of a firm's economic activities and is prepared on a quarterly, semi-annual, or annual basis. These results are communicated through financial statements which include the balance sheet, profit and loss statement, income and expenses accounts, cash flow statements, and notes to the financial statements and narratives. These accounts help the investing public decide to make investment decisions and are subject to external audit as may be required by provider of capital or regulator.

Managerial accounting is a more detailed reporting system as it is used by the management in its day-to-day decision-making. Managerial accounting thus looks at the areas of planning, control, decision-making, performance measurement, and evaluation, which is used by its internal users to reduce costs and maximize profits.

Elements of General Purpose Financial Statements: Assets, Liabilities, Owner's Equity, Revenues, and Expenses

The assets, liabilities, and owners' equity for the balance sheet are represented by the following equation:

$$\text{ASSETS} = \text{CAPITAL} + \text{LIABILITES}.$$

The revenue, expenses, and net profit in the income statement are represented by the following equation:

$$\text{NET PROFIT} = \text{REVENUE} \quad \text{EXPENSES}$$

Business transactions are classified into the following five categories:

Assets These are resources owned by the business and listed in the balance sheet. In the financial statements assets are put into two categories: current assets and fixed assets. Current assets include cash, receivables, inventory, and investments for sale. These values change daily as the entity conducts business. Fixed assets are held and used by the company over a number of years. These include land and building, furniture, equipment, and motor vehicles.

Liabilities These are claims against the resources of the business and represent monies the company owes to third parties and include loans taken by the business, accounts payable or creditors (organizations that the business buys goods on credit), and accruals. These are expenses the business has incurred during the accounting period, and which remain unpaid at the end of the period. Accruals for rent and electricity are good examples as these are paid in arrears. Where a supplier's invoice is not received before the accounts are closed, an accrual for the expense will be made. This is the application of the matching concept and ensures the accuracy of the financial statements—that is all revenues and expenses are recorded in the period in which it occurs.

Liabilities are generally included in current liabilities except for long-term loans which are reclassified in to current, medium, and long-term portions accordingly.

Owner's equity is the owners claim against the resources of the business. It represents the owner's investment in the business plus all retained profits, that is profits after dividend payments. This forms part of the capital of the company. For a sole trader or partnership, amounts withdrawn from the company are deducted from this capital account and referred to as drawings.

Let's say Harry started a business with $200,000 in 2015. He made a profit of $35,000 for that year, and he made no drawings from the business. In 2016 he made a profit of $25,000 and he made drawings totaling $5000. In 2017 he made $25,000 profit and again had drawings of $5000. This would be his capital account balances for the three years:

Years	2015 ($)	2016 ($)	2017 ($)
Opening capital	200, 000	235,000	255,000
Add: Net profit	35,000	25,000	25,000
	235,000	260,000	280,000
Less: Drawings	0	5000	5000
Closing capital	235,000	255,000	275,000

For a partnership the capital accounts would be disaggregated to represent the individual transactions of each partner.

Revenue are resources earned by the business from its operations during a given accounting period. So fees earned, sales, services rendered, interest and rent are all revenues.

Expenses are the costs incurred during the accounting period to generate revenue. They include salaries, wages, electricity, telephone, water, advertising, transportation, insurance, marketing, printing, depreciation (which is an expense even though it does not result in an outlay of cash, but rather the use of the asset during the period), and rent. All expenses go in the income and expenses account. Net profit is the total revenue for the period less expenses.

For example if you have Electricity of $1,000 but $200 of this amount represents a prepayment for the next year, then the electricity figure in the income statement would be $1000 less $200 or $800. So prepayments are deducted from the utility amounts to give the expense that would have been incurred in that period.

Similarly if you had $1,000 electricity payments in 2008 but you used $1,200 worth of electricity, so $200 was left unpaid or is an accrual at the end of the period then we add that $200. So $1,200 would be the amount representing electricity expenses in the income statement, since that is the amount used in the accounting period.

So in the income statement the electricity expense would be reduced by the prepayments in the first instance of 200 resulting in an electricity expense of 1000. Similarly where all the expenses are not paid within the current year, any unpaid amounts for expenses incurred in the current year must be accrued.

The Accounting Cycle/Process

The accounting process is a series of activities or transactions that ends with each being recorded in the books of entry, each transaction having debit and credit entries which must agree in total. An accounting period is usually one year; however, accounts may be prepared quarterly or semiannually and management accounts are usually prepared monthly or as frequently as necessary. At the end of each financial period, financial statements are prepared. The process or cycle in the preparation of financial statements includes the following procedures:

1. *Analyze the transactions:* Each source document is analyzed to determine the substance of the transaction to determine the accounts to be debited and credited. Each transaction has a twofold effect; that is, it will increase one of the items in the accounting equation (Assets = Capital + Liabilities) while it will decrease another item.
2. *Preparation of journals:* After the accounts affected are determined and classified then the transaction is recorded in the appropriate journal or books of original entry as follows:

   - Sales Journal—used to record credit sales;
   - Purchases Journal—used to record credit purchases;
   - Returns Inwards Journal—to record goods that are returned to the firm after they have been sold;
   - Returns Outwards Journal—to record goods that are returned by the firm after they have been purchased;
   - Cash Book—to record receipts and payments of cash and check;
   - General Journal—to record all other transactions.

3. *Post to ledger:* After the transactions are entered into the relevant journal a process called "posting the transaction" occurs; that is, the amounts in the journal are placed in the debit or credit of the account as detailed in the journal. As with journals similar accounts are grouped in one ledger or book, so there are different ledgers in which similar accounts are kept. Some examples are as follows:

   - Sales Ledger–for recording customers' (credit) personal accounts;
   - Purchases Ledger—for suppliers' (credit) personal accounts;
   - General Ledger—contains the remaining double entry accounts such as expenses, fixed assets, capital, and so on.

Stages (1)–(3) are performed continuously during the accounting period, most times in batches and are repeated until the end of the accounting period at which time a trial balance is prepared which must be in balance and the same is reviewed and analyzed to determine if any errors occurred so it may be corrected before the financial statements are prepared.

4. *Prepare unadjusted trial balance:* After the transactions are posted to the ledgers at the end of the accounting period, the **individual accounts are balanced and their balances are extracted and entered into a trial balance** which lists all the credit and debit balances. The importance of this rests in the double entry principle. If for every transaction there was a debit and corresponding credit entry then the trial balance MUST balance; that is the credit balances must equal the debit balances.
5. *Adjustments:* If the trial balance does not balance then there are recording, posting, or arithmetical errors, which must be identified and **the error adjusted** using the same stages outlined above, through journal and ledger entries. Interestingly even if the Trial Balance is in balance, that is the total debits equal the total credits, there may still be errors such as compensating errors, errors of omission, commission, and duplication. These errors may be found through analysis of variances, retracing of transactiona and review of individual accounts and are corrected like the other errors, through journal entries.

   Adjustments are also necessary at the end of the accounting period given the accrual system of accounting. This system is the one most widely used as it takes into account all revenue earned and all expenses incurred during the accounting period ensuring the matching of revenue and expenses. In accordance with this principle adjustments and journal entries are needed for accruals and prepayments.
6. *Prepare the adjusted trial balance:* The adjusted balances of the accounts are then re-entered into an adjusted trial balance or a worksheet or if computerized an adjusted trial balance is automatically prepared.
7. *Prepare financial statements:* After the adjusted trial balance is reviewed and analyzed the following financial statements can be prepared:

   - Income Statement—represents all revenues less all expenditure and shows either a net profit or a net loss;
   - Balance Sheet—reflects the accounting equation showing assets against the liabilities and owners' equity;
   - A cash flow statement may also be produced using additional information from other statements.

8. *Closing Journal Entries:* After the statements are produced closing journal entries are made to close temporary accounts such as revenues, expenses, gains, and losses. The closing process entails:

   - Identifying the accounts for closing;
   - Recording and posting the closing entries;
   - Preparing a post-closing trial balance for the balances of permanent accounts.

9. *Interpret and analyze financial statements*: Stakeholders and potential investors use the financial statements to analyze the company's performance using ratio analysis. Ratios such as Rate of Return or Net profit on Capital Employed, Profitability, and Liquidity can be calculated to give an indication of the company's performance in the current year and the same is compared with prior years and of other companies.

This entire process is repeated in every accounting period and is defined as the accounting process/cycle in the diagram below (Fig. 9.1).

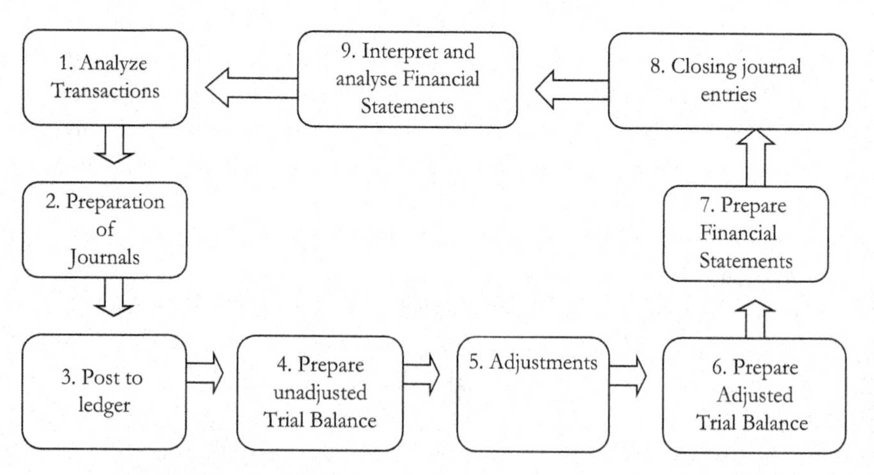

Fig. 9.1 The accounting process/cycle

The Double Entry Principle

The double entry principle states that for every transaction there must be equal debit entry/entries and a corresponding credit entry/entries. This may be termed a simple entry. A compound entry is when there are more than one debit and credit entries but the total debits must be equal to the total credits. This demonstrates the twofold nature of each transaction (resources vs. claim/expenditure). This principle is also referred to as the dual aspect concept and is used to ensure that the equality of the accounting equation is maintained after recording each transaction or event.

Debits and Credits

Debits and credits are tools used by the accountant to increase or decrease account balances. A debit entry is made on the left side of the "T" account and a credit entry is made on the right side of the "T" account. By convention, asset and expense accounts normally carry "Debit" balances. Liabilities, Owner's Equity, and Revenue accounts normally carry "Credit" balances.

Rule: All accounts with normal debit balances are increased by debit entries and decreased by credit entries. Conversely, accounts with normal credit balances are increased by credit entries and decreased by debit entries.

Example: Co. X purchases a motor vehicle by cash for $340,000.

The journal entries would be:

1.	DR Motor vehicle	340,000	
	CR Cash		340,000

To record the cash purchase of motor vehicle. The journal is posted to the Motor Vehicle account and Cash account in the general ledger. This is referred to as a "t-account" which is a graphic representation of the general ledger account. The name of the account is placed above the "T". Debit entries are shown on the left and credit entries on the right.

The T-accounts that would be affected (Fig. 9.2):

Motor Vehicle

DR		CR	
Cash	340,000		

Cash

DR		CR	
		Motor Vehicle	340,000

Fig. 9.2 The T-accounts that would be affected

The motor vehicle T-account has been debited since it is an asset and the cash account has been depleted by the purchase of motor vehicle for the sum of $340,000 and the account is credited.

Trial Balance

A trial balance is a listing of all accounts in the General Ledger. It is usually arranged in the chart of account sequence and is used to determine whether the accounting records are in balance. The trial balance, therefore, verifies the mathematical accuracy of the various transactions posted to the accounting records. This is in keeping with the double entry principle of accounting.

Equality in the trial balance does not always ensure accuracy. There are several errors that result in inaccuracies in the General Ledger which do not affect the balancing of the trial balance. They include the following:

Errors of Omission This happens when a transaction is not entered in the accounting records. Neither of the double entry entries are made, for example, a firm purchased a motor vehicle for $85,000 on credit but the necessary debit entry (computers) and credit entry (accounts payable) were not posted to the General ledger. Hence the transaction was completely omitted from the accounting records. This frequently occurs for credit transactions as there is no payment of cash.

Errors of Duplication This occurs when a transaction is entered more than once in the accounting records. This is the primary reason why original documents and not copies of documents are used in recording transactions. This avoids duplication.

Compensatory Errors This occurs when two or more errors offset each other. For example, assume that ABC posted cash received from BCD Co. of $6500 as $1500 to BCD Co.'s account and posted revenue earned of $11,500 to revenue account as $6000. Note that the $5000 understatement of the debit cash entry is compensated by the $5000 understatement of the credit (revenue) entry. To correct this account you debit cash with $5000 (to compensate for the understatement of revenue) and then credit the revenue account with $5000.

Errors of Original Entry This occurs when transactions are incorrectly entered in the General Journal. For example, assume that ABC Co. posted a credit sale that was initially recorded as $20,400 in the General Journal as $20,900 in the General Ledger. The entry that would have been made was credit sales $20,900 and debit debtors/accounts receivable $20,900. So to correct the error in posting we need to prepare a journal and debit sales $500 and credit debtors $500.

Posting to the Wrong Account This would require the reversal of the original entry and posting to the correct accounts.

Errors of Classification Certain capital items may be classified as repair and maintenance expense. For example, assume that cupboards purchased for use in the business were classified as an expense which will have a direct impact on the profit and loss account. This would also require a reversal of the entry and posting to the correct general ledger account.

Unequal Totals in the Trial Balance

Where the trial balance totals do not balance, attempts should be made to locate the error. However most systems are computerized and there are several input controls which minimize this.

The following process is useful for the location of errors in an unbalanced trial balance:

1. Add the trial balance columns once more;
2. Calculate the difference between the debit and credit totals. If the difference is divisible by 9, the problem may be caused by a:

   (i) Transposition—reversal of two digits of a given number (e.g., $345 is recorded as $453);
   (ii) Slide—improper movement of the decimal point to the left or to the right (e.g., $447 is recorded as $44.70)

3. Calculate one-half difference between the debt and credit totals, and if the amount can be located in the trial balance, a debit amount may have been entered in the credit column or vice versa.

Multiperiod costs and revenue must be split among two or more accounting periods. These include prepayments and accruals.

(a) *Prepaid Expenses*

These are expenses paid in the current financial (reporting) period but which will provide benefits in two or more subsequent periods. Prepaid expenses are classified as assets until the benefits are realized and subsequently treated as expenses in the period in which they are consumed. These include items paid on a periodic basis such as insurance, electricity, and rent. When the benefits are realized, an adjusting journal entry is made to debit the expense account and credit the prepayment account.

For instance, assume that ABC paid insurance premium of $12,000 on October 1, 2016, for the next 12 months. The firm's financial year ends on December 31, 2016. How would XYZ account for this transaction?

On October 1, 2016, XYZ would record the following entry in the journal:

Oct. 1	DR Prepaid insurance	$12,000	
	CR Cash		$12,000
	To record insurance paid for the period 1st October, 2016 to 30th September, 2017		

On December 31, 2016, three months of insurance coverage would have been used and XYZ would record the following adjusting entry:

Dec. 31	DR Insurance expense	$3000	
	CR Prepaid insurance		$3000
	To record insurance expense for the period 1st October to 31st December, 2016		

*(The calculation—$12,000/12 will give you $1000 a month. So for three months used October to December $1000*3 = 3000)*

It must be noted that the adjusting entry will affect both the income statement and the balance sheet.

(b) *Fixed Assets*

Fixed assets generate revenue to the business over an extended period. Owing to the matching principle, the costs of assets are initially recorded at cost and depreciation is charged to the profit and loss account based on the useful life of the asset less the residual value of the asset if any. The asset decreases in value over the life of the asset and this reduction is called depreciation.

Depreciation is defined as the systematic allocation of the cost of a fixed asset to the financial periods benefiting from its use and can be calculated in a number of ways. One of the most common methods is the straight line method. The formula is as follows:

$$\text{Annual depreciation expense} = \frac{\text{Acquisition cost}\left(\text{cost of asset}\right) - \text{Estimated residual value}}{\text{Estimated useful life}\left(\text{in years}\right)}$$

The cost of the asset includes the initial purchase price plus all costs to bring the asset to its present position and location. Fixed assets are generally recorded in certain categories such as land and buildings, machinery and equipment, furniture and fittings, motor vehicles, and other specific classes.

Depreciation expense is recorded by debiting the depreciation expense account and crediting the accumulated depreciation account. Fixed assets are reported in the balance sheet at net book value. However the notes to the financial statements provide a schedule of fixed assets details all brought forward cost of assets, additions, disposals, and closing balance. The schedule also includes the accumulated depreciation brought forward plus current year depreciation less adjustments. The net book value is the total assets less the accumulated depreciation.

For example let us assume that ABC Co. recently purchased a van for \$20,000. ABC estimates that the van has a useful life of five years and a residual value of \$5000. What is the annual depreciation expense and the net book value at the end of one year?

$$\text{The annual depreciation expense is}: \frac{\$20{,}000 - \$5000}{5} = \$3000$$

Note in the straight line method of depreciation that the annual depreciation expense will remain the same throughout the useful life of the asset. Note also that it is assumed that after the five useful years the asset would be sold at the residual value.

The depreciation expense for year one is recorded as follows:

Dec. 31	DR Depreciation expense	\$3000	
	CR Accumulated depreciation		\$3000
	To record depreciation expense		

This depreciation expense is an expense to be included under expenses in the income statement.

The net book value of ABC's van at the end of one year that would be recorded in the balance sheet is:

Acquisition cost	$20,000
Less: accumulated depreciation	*($3000)*
Net book value	$17,000

After two years the net book value will be $20,000 minus $6000 = $14,000.

(c) *Unearned Revenues (Deferred revenues)*

This is represented as a liability account that reports amounts received in advance of providing a good or service. Unearned revenues are recorded by debiting the cash account (an asset) and crediting the unearned revenue account (a liability). When the revenue is subsequently earned, an adjusting entry is made to reclassify the unearned revenue as revenue. This is done by debiting the unearned revenue account and crediting the revenue account.

Example: Assume that ABC collected cash amounting to $50,000 on October 31, 2016, for service that will be provided during the following financial year. The firm's year end is December 31. How will the transaction be recorded initially and what will be the adjusting entry needed on December 31, 2016?

The journal entry on October 31, 2016, will be:

Oct. 31	DR Cash	$50,000	
	CR Unearned revenue		$50,000
	To record cash received but revenue not yet earned for the financial year 2016		

Then on December 31, 2017, when the revenue has been earned the following adjusting entry is made to record revenue earned for the financial year ended 31st December, 2017:

Dec. 31	DR Unearned revenue	$50,000	
	CR Revenue		$50,000

(d) *Accrued Expenses*

These are expenses that have been incurred but not yet paid or entered into the accounting records. Expenses that frequently fall into this category include salaries, wages, interest, and taxes which may be due by the end of the financial period but have not yet been paid.

Example: Assume that XYZ's workers should be paid wages $2000 for three days on December 31, 2011, but will not be paid until the end of the workweek which falls in January 2012. What adjusting entry is recorded on December 31, 2011, the end of XYZ's financial year:

Dec. 31	DR Wages expense	2000	
	CR Wages payable		2000
	To record wages payable at December 31, 2011		

(e) *Accrued Revenues*

Accrued revenues represent revenues earned during the current financial period but not yet received. Typical examples include interest due from the bank, commissions earned and not yet received, and income earned but not yet billed. Accrued revenues are recorded by debiting a receivable account (asset) and crediting a revenue account.

Example: Assume that ABC has provided consultancy services worth $20,000 to a client during the financial year ended December 31, 2016. The client has not yet been billed and ABC is about to prepare its financial statements.

The Journal entries:

Dec. 31	DR Service revenue receivable	$20,000	
	CR Service revenue		$20,000
	Being revenue earned but not yet received as at 31st December, 2016		

Note once again that both the balance sheet (service revenue receivable) and the income statement (revenue) are affected. Adjusting journal entries are also recorded to correct errors in the accounting system.

Examples to practice adjusting entries. Assume that ABC is preparing its financial statements for the year ended December 31, 2016, and the following information has been provided:

1. Wages owed to employees: $6000;
2. Interest due from bank: $1200;
3. Previously unearned revenue earned during the period: $15,000;
4. Prepaid insurance expired during the period: $2500;
5. Utilities due not yet paid: $3000;
6. Depreciation expenses on computer: $1600;
7. Office supplies used during the year: $4000 (previously recorded as an asset);
8. Services provided but not yet billed: $7000;
9. Salaries due to employees but not yet paid: $9000;
10. Rent income not yet received: $2000.

The following adjusting entries will have to be made for the above information:

All entries on the journal would be made at December 31:

(i)	DR Wages expense	6000	
	CR Wages payable		6000
(ii)	DR Interest receivable	1200	
	CR Interest revenue		1200
(iii)	DR Unearned revenue	15,000	
	CR Revenue		15,000
(iv)	DR Insurance expense	2500	
	CR Prepaid insurance		2500
(v)	DR Utilities expense	3000	
	CR Utilities payable		3000
(vi)	DR Depreciation expense	1600	
	CR Accumulated dep.		1600
(vii)	DR Office supplies expense	4000	
	CR Office supplies		4000
(viii)	DR Accounts receivable	7000	
	CR Service revenue		7000
(ix)	DR Salaries expense	9000	
	CR Salaries payable		9000
(x)	DR Rent receivable	2000	
	CR Rent revenue		2000

Analysis and Interpretation of Financial Statements

Financial statement analysis is one of the best ways of understanding the company's performance relative to previous years and others companies and the industry in which it operates. The analyst is also concerned with the financial position and results of operations and the relationship among various items in the balance sheet and income statement. The use of ratios is important to get a fuller understanding of the financial statements. The different ratios are used to evaluate the financial position, the profitability, and the future prospects of the business. The use of ratios therefore requires intelligent analysis of financial statements. The three widely used standards of comparison are absolute standards, industry standards, and comparative standards.

Comparisons in the form of ratio analysis are significant for the purpose of evaluating the company's performance. Ratios of financial statements must be also compared with industry standards. Absolute standards provide a rule of thumb and allows proper comparisons and interpretations thereto.

When analyzing the ratios of a firm always make reference to the rule of thumb for each ratio and compare the firm's ratios with the ratios of the previous years and with other firms in the industry.

Liquidity Ratios

Liquidity ratios measure the short-term obligations of a firm. Liquidity ratios are used to determine the company's ability to meet its short-term commitments and are important ratios for lenders of the business who need payments usually on a monthly basis.

Both the current ratio and the quick ratio can be used to gauge a company's liquidity. If the merchandise/inventory that the company holds or is involved in trading can easily be converted into cash, then the current ratio is a better indicator of liquidity. If, however, the inventory cannot easily be converted into cash then the quick ratio is the better indicator.

$$1.\quad \text{Current ratio} = \frac{\text{Current assets}}{\text{Current liabilities}}$$

The current ratio is one important measure used to evaluate a company's ability to pay its short-term obligations.

If the ratio is less than 1 then this means that the company's current liabilities exceed its current assets and would face problems covering its current liabilities. Even if a company's current ratio is greater than 1 the ratio needs to be compared with the industry's norm to get a better idea of the liquidity of the firm. However a current ratio of more than 1 generally indicates that the company can meet its short-term obligations.

$$2.\quad \text{Acid test ratio}: \frac{\text{Quick assets}\left(\begin{array}{c}\text{Cash plus receivables}\\ \text{(Stock \& prepayments are not included)}\end{array}\right)}{\text{Current liabilities}}$$

Another measure that is used to assess a company's ability to pay its current liabilities is the acid test ratio. The acid test ratio differs from the current ratio by excluding less liquid assets such as inventory. Liquidity refers to how quickly an item is converted to cash. The less liquid assets are those that will take longer to be converted to cash. The acid test ratio is also called the quick ratio.

The rule of thumb for liquidity ratio is 1. An acid test ratio of less than 1 suggests a potential liquidity problem unless the company can generate enough cash from sales and the accounts payable. Similarly a value greater than 1 can hide a liquidity problem if payables are due shortly and receivables are not collected until late in the next period.

Equity Ratios

These ratios measure the contributions of shareholders (as compared with the financing provided by the firm's creditors). The shareholders' equity ratio provides complementary information by expressing total equity as a percentage of total assets. This shows the percentage of the company's assets contributed by the shareholders as opposed to its debtors/creditors. A company is considered less risky if its capital structure contains more equity than debts. The greater the stockholder financing (equity), the more losses a company can absorb through equity before the assets become inadequate to satisfy the claims of creditors.

$$\text{Shareholder's equity ratio} = \frac{\text{Shareholders' equity}}{\text{Total assets}}$$

Companies are financed by equity and debt. There must be a good balance between debt and equity so the debtholder feels less at risk owing to the substantial investment of the shareholder. Debt also carries copulsory interest cost and interst cover is another ratio of interest to the debtholder.

A shareholder's equity ratio in excess of 50% is preferred as it signifies that the shareholders contribute more to the company and it is less leveraged.

Activity Ratios

Activity ratios help complement the liquidity ratios. They tell us how effectively the firm is employing its resources.

1. $$\text{Accounts receivable turnover} = \frac{\text{Net credit sales}}{\text{Average receivable before deduction of allowances}}$$

This ratio thus tells us how often a company converts its average accounts receivable into cash during the accounting period. For example, an accounts receivable turnover of 15 means that in that accounting period debtors would have paid their debts 15 times over. This ratio reflects on the effectiveness of the company's credit policy and the managerial effectiveness in maintaining credit controls.

2. $$\text{No. of days' sales uncollected} = \frac{360}{\text{Turnover of receivables}}$$

This ratio is used in conjunction with the above ratio and it indicates how quickly a company can convert its accounts receivable into cash. This ratio computes the length of time on average the firm must wait after making a credit sale before receiving cash. Again for this ratio to be useful it needs to be compared with the industry average.

Two other ratios, which are used to measure both activity and stock management, are the inventory turnover ratio and the number of days required to turnover the inventory.

3. $$\text{Inventory turnover} = \frac{\text{Cost of goods sold}}{\text{Average finished goods inventory}}$$

This ratio measures the number of times a company sells its average level of inventory during a year. This ratio is a good indicator of how well management is controlling inventory but also gives an indication of short-term liquidity since it shows how many times inventory is converted into sales. If the ratio is low compared to the industry standard then the company's turnover is slow which can result in obsolescence and reduced profitability. It may also be that the company has problems converting inventory into sales and cash. It can also mean that the company is holding too much inventory which may affect its liquidity standing. A high ratio means the company converts inventory quickly into sales. Too high a ratio however may result in loss of sales and profits as the firm holds inadequate inventory resulting in stock outs.

4. $$\text{No. of days required to turnover inventory} = \frac{360}{\text{Inventory turnover}}$$

5. $$\text{Fixed asset turnover} = \frac{\text{Sales}}{\text{Net fixed assets}\left(\begin{array}{c}\text{Cost of asset minus}\\ \text{accumulated depreciation}\end{array}\right)}$$

This ratio measures the sales generated per dollar of fixed assets. Therefore, this ratio indicates the efficiency with which the firm has been using its fixed assets to generate sales.

$$\text{Total asset turnover} = \frac{\text{Sales}}{\text{Total assets}}$$

This ratio indicates the efficiency with which the firm uses its assets to generate sales. Generally a higher ratio is indicative that the assets are more efficiently utilized.

Profitability Ratios

Calculating profitability ratios are useful for all stakeholders in a company, the management, present, past and future stakeholders. This gives a good indication of the company's viability and the efficiency of management.

$$1. \quad \text{Net income as a \% of net sales} = \frac{\text{Net income}}{\text{Net sales}}$$

This ratio represents the amount of profit in every dollar of sales. This ratio needs to be compared with the industry's average and the past ratios of the company.

$$2. \quad \text{Net income as a return on shareholder's equity} \\ (\text{return on equity}): \frac{\text{Net income}}{\text{Shareholders' equity}}$$

This ratio represents the return on shareholders' investment in the company. It can be compared with returns from other investment opportunities.

3. $$\text{Earnings per common share} = \frac{\text{Net income accruing to common shareholders}}{\text{Common shares outstanding}}$$

This ratio represents the amount of income earned by each share of a company. This aids investors in their valuation of common shares. It is especially useful when compared to the market price of the share as it reveals information about the stock market's expectation for the company's future growth in earnings, dividends, and other opportunities.

4. $$\text{Price earnings ratio} = \frac{\text{Market value per common share}}{\text{Earnings per common share}}$$

It is possible to make a comparison of the rate of return by dividing the earnings per common share by the market value of the common share. Some analysts interpret this ratio as what the price the market is willing to pay for the current earnings of the company (or in other words what the market is willing to pay for the share as compared to the price the share is selling for in the market).

5. $$\text{Gross profit margin} = \frac{\text{Gross profit}}{\text{Net sales}}$$

This ratio represents the gross margin in each dollar of sales. Gross profit= net sales – cost of goods sold. This ratio represents the financial health of the business. It gives the company's ability to cover expenses (outside of direct cost of goods) and to save money.

10

Business Planning

A business plan is a written document that describes a business. It covers objectives, strategies, sales, marketing, and financial forecasts. A business plan has many functions, provides a road map, helps to secure external funding, identifies goals and strategies. A business plan is a written summary of an entrepreneur's proposed business venture. A business plan comprises the following elements: an executive summary, description of the business, marketing, competition, operating procedures, personnel, and financial data. As the business grows and economic and other conditions change, the business plan will require updating and changing. It is a living organism, always changing in response to the environment and market forces.

Reasons for Writing a Business Plan

A business plan should be a tool to run and grow the business; something you continue to use and refine over time. A business plan should be as precise as possible as an excessively long business plan can be a huge hassle to deal with and often finds itself in a desk drawer, never to be seen again. Business plans should clearly define what the business does and a

C. Sahadeo, *Financial Literacy and Money Script*,
https://doi.org/10.1007/978-3-319-77075-8_10

key message that explains why the business is uniquely qualified to succeed. A business plan forces the leader to have a stated vision and mission, to set goals, forecast of sales, growth and expansion. Similarly based on estimated prices, expenses and a review of controllable cost, goals must also be set for revenue and net profit. Creating goals is the first step to achieving them. Goal setting clearly yields superior results and developing a habit of setting goals will help grow the business in a sustainable manner.

The preparation of a written business plan is not the end result of the planning process. The operationalization and realization of that plan is the ultimate goal. However, the writing of the plan is an important intermediate stage—*failing to plan can mean planning to fail.* For an established business it demonstrates that careful consideration has been given to the development of the business, and for a start-up it shows that the entrepreneur has done his homework. A business plan articulates the vision and future plans of the firm. It is important for the management team and more particularly for a new venture. Investors and other external stakeholders such as investors, potential business partners, and employees are users of the business plan. A firm must validate the feasibility of its business idea, develop an effective business model, and have a good understanding of its competitive environment (by preparing a SWOT analysis) prior to presenting its business plan to others.

The best person to write a business plan is the owner of the business. It is essentially the entrepreneur's dream being realized and its stakeholders, investors, lenders, customers, vendors, managers, and employees are relying on the owner's leadership to deliver the results of the business plan. By preparing the business plan it also demonstrates that the entrepreneur takes ownership. The leader is also the best person to convey the vision and mission of the organization. Of course, the assistance of experts in the respective areas is always recommended.

Preparing a satisfactory business plan is a painful but essential exercise. The planning process forces leaders and entrepreneurs to identify what they want to achieve, and how and when they can do it. A business plan can play a vital role in helping to avoid mistakes and identifying hidden opportunities. The process of planning, that is, thinking, discussing, researching, and analyzing is just as, or even more, important than the final plan.

A clearly written and attractively packaged business plan will make it easier to interest possible supporters, investors, and employees. A well-prepared business plan will demonstrate that the leader knows the business and that they have thought through its development in terms of products, management, finances, and, most importantly, markets and competition.

Start with a Business Strategy

In developing a strategic plan, it is desirable to clearly identify the current status, objectives, and strategies of an existing business or the latest thinking in respect of a new venture. Correctly defined, these can be used as the basis for a critical examination or SWOT (strength, weaknesses, opportunities, and threats) analysis. This then leads to strategy development covering the following areas:

- Vision
- Mission
- Objectives
- Values
- Strategies
- Goals
- Programs
- Financial projections

Vision

The first step is to develop a realistic vision for the business. This is a description of what an organization would like to achieve or accomplish and should be presented as a picture of the business in three or more years in terms of its likely operations, physical appearance, size, and activities.

Mission

A mission statement is a statement of an organization's purpose. The nature of a business is often expressed in terms of its mission which indicates the type and scope of the business, its products and services, its primary customers or market, and can be described, for example, "to design, develop, manufacture, and market specific product lines for sale on the basis of certain features to meet the identified needs of specified customer groups via certain distribution channels in particular geographic areas." A statement along these lines indicates what the business is about and is infinitely clearer than saying, for instance, "we're in electronics" or "we are in business to make money" (assuming that the business is not a mint!). Also, some people confuse mission statements with value statements: the former should be very specific while the latter can deal with "softer" issues surrounding the business.

Objectives

The third key element is to explicitly state the objectives of the business in terms of the results it plans or wants to achieve in the medium to long term. Aside from presumably indicating a necessity to achieve regular profits (expressed as return on shareholders' funds), objectives should relate to the expectations and requirements of all the major stakeholders, including employees, and should reflect the underlying reasons for running the business.

Values

The next element to address is the values governing the operation of the business and its conduct or relationships with society, customers, and its employees. Decisions of a company must be made in line with its values; for example, if quality is one of the company's values, when a product or service is off standard, the product should be rejected and corrective action taken to eliminate the error. Clearly enunciated values of an organization must be demonstrated and communicated from the top. This assists in the branding of the entity and building a positive image. Values of a company can change with time as the company continues along a drive of continuous improvement and excellence. Typical values can include integrity, commitment, customer focus, and innovation.

Strategies

Strategies are the policies and guidelines by which the mission, vision, and objectives may be developed and achieved. They can cover the business as a whole including diversification, organic growth, or acquisition plans, or they can relate to primary matters in key functional areas. Some examples are as follows:

- *All growth and expansion will be funded internally.*
- *New products will replace existing ones over the next three to five years.*
- *All assembly work will be contracted out to lower the company's break-even point.*

Goals

These are specific interim or ultimate time-based measurements to be achieved by implementing strategies in pursuit of the company's objectives—for example, to achieve sales of $5 million in five years' time.

Programs

The final elements are the programs which set out the implementation plans for the key strategies. It is important that the mission, objectives, values, strategies, and goals are interlinked and consistent with each other.

Preparatory Business Planning Issues

Before any detailed work commences on writing a comprehensive business plan, the following issues must be considered:

- Determine the product/service the company will be offering, including any particular features of the item;
- Clearly identify and define the target audience;
- Identify the unique characteristics of the product and service offered;
- Map out the plan's structure (contents page);
- Decide on the likely length of the plan; and
- Identify all the main issues to be addressed.

Develop an Outline Business Plan

Start by peparing an outline (a table of contents will help) of the plan. Having devised the basic outline of the business plan, the next task is to expand this to include subheadings and appendices. This extended structure should be critically reviewed to ensure that all the salient elements of the plan are included and that it has a logical flow. This approach should also ensure that the plan has an appropriate level of detail and is correctly targeted at its audience, investors, directors/shareholders, financial institutions, and employees.

Guidelines for Writing a Business Plan

1. Structure of the business plan. To make the best impression, a business plan should follow a conventional structure. Although some entrepreneurs want to demonstrate creativity, departing from the basic structure is usually a mistake. Typically, investors are very busy people and want a plan that can easily provide the critical information the investor needs to make a decision, that is, whether to invest or not! There are many software packages available that employ an interactive, menu-driven approach to assist in the writing of a business plan. Some of these programs are very helpful.

2. Content of the business plan. The business plan should give clear and concise information on all the important aspects of the proposed venture. For most plans, 25–30 pages are sufficient.
3. Style or format of the business plan. The appearance of a business plan is important. There are three types of business plans:

   (i) *Summary plan*: A summary business plan is 10–15 pages and can be very effective if carefully prepared.
   (ii) *Full business plan*: A full business plan provides a detailed analysis of the business and its strategies and is typically 25–35 pages long.
   (iii) *Operational business plan*: This is primarily for an internal audience and is very useful in reviewing and documenting systems. It is usually between 40 and 100 pages long.

Outline of the Business Plan

A specific firm's business plan may vary, depending on the nature of the business and the personalities of the founding entrepreneurs. A business plan is a key tool for entrepreneurs to determine whether to start a business or not and is necessary if seeking external funding. It also helps the entrepreneur to organize ideas that will convert plans to action for starting up the business. A business plan is also required by investors such as banks and the equity partners. Existing business owners can also prepare a business plan to assist in the growth and development of the company.

Elements of the Business Plan

1. Cover page and Table of Contents. The cover page and table of contents should include the name of the company, its address, its phone number, the date, and contact information for the lead entrepreneur.
2. Executive summary. The executive summary is a short overview of the entire business plan. It introduces the business model and describes the key products and markets. It should list the key personnel and the experience they bring, as well as summary financial infor-

mation. The business plan provides a busy reader with everything that needs to be known about the new venture's distinctive nature. Although the executive summary appears at the beginning of the business plan, it should be prepared after the plan is completed. An executive summary should not exceed two single-spaced pages. The recommended format for an executive summary is an overview of the business plan on a section-by-section basis.

3. Industry analysis. It is important that a full understanding of the industry in which the firm is operating is studied, analyzed and understood. Before selecting its target market, a business should have a good grasp on its industry and prepare a SWOT analysis. This would assist the leader in developing strategies to counteract its weaknesses and threats and strategies to capitalize on its strengths and opportunities. Other useful tools to assist with this are Porter's Five Forces and the PESTLE analysis which looks at Political, Economic, Social, Technological, Legal, and Environmental factors that could impact the business. Knowledge of the industry includes industry size, growth rate and sales projections, industry structure, nature of participants, key success factors, industry trends, and long-term prospects. Industry trends should be analyzed which include both environmental and business trends. This is arguably the most important section of an industry analysis because it often lays the foundation for a new business idea in a given industry.
4. Company description. This details the location of its operations and may describe the vision and direction of the company. Although at first glance this section may seem less critical than the others, it is extremely important. It should include the following:
   (a) The company description should start with a brief introduction which provides an overview of the company.
   (b) It may also include company history, vision statement, mission statement, values, products and services, current status, legal status and ownership, and key partnerships.
5. Market analysis. While the industry analysis focuses on the industry that a firm will participate in, the market analysis breaks the industry

into segments and zeroes in on the specific segment (or target market) to which the firm will target. The market analysis will include market segmentation and target market selection, buyer behavior, and competitor analysis. Market segmentation is the process of dividing the market into distinct segments. Markets can be segmented in many ways, such as geography, demographic variables, psychographic variables, and products. A competitor analysis is critical to determine the company's strategy to ensure it differentiates its products and services from the market wherever possible.

6. Economics of the business. This section begins the financial analysis of the business, which is further detailed in the financial projections. It addresses the basic assumptions of how profits are earned and its "break even", that is, how many units of a business's product or service must be sold for the business to start earning a profit. The following analyses and worksheets must be prepared as follows:

    (a) Revenue drivers and profit margins must be identified and determined from the onset. Identify and describe the size of the overall gross margins and margins for each of the major revenue drivers of the business. The weighted average contribution margins can now be determined and used in scenario planning for various levels of production.
    (b) The fixed and variable costs need to be detailed in a monthly schedule.
    (c) Operating leverage and its implications: Analyze all expenditure to determine whether the costs are predominantly fixed or variable as these have implications for cost reduction and strategies thereto.
    (d) Start-up costs: Distinguish the one-time start-up costs of the business and list these separately to determine the one-off start-up capital and funding required.
    (e) Overall economic model: Prepare various simulations on the data from the previous analyses and prepare projected profit and loss statements and balance sheets.
    (f) Break-even chart and calculations: Compute the number of units the business has to sell to "break even" prior to earning a profit based on the different assumptions adopted.

(g) Profitability: Address the issue of how solid or vulnerable the profit stream appears to be, with a series of scenarios or "what if's"

7. Marketing plan. The marketing plan focuses on how the business will market and sell its product or service. It deals with the nuts and bolts of marketing in terms of product, price, promotion, distribution, and sales and in particular the use of social media to grow sales exponentially. A firm's marketing strategy refers to its overall approach for marketing its products and services, how it positions itself in its market, and how it differentiates itself from its competitors. The plan should deal with the company's approach to the four P's, that is, place, product, price, promotion, and should describe the company's sales process or cycle and specific sales tactics it will employ.
8. Product (or service) design and development plan. If a new product or service is being developed the plan must include the status of the development efforts. The stages of development are product conception, prototyping, initial production, and full production. The plan should describe specifically the point at which the product or service is at and provide a timeline that describes the remaining steps.
9. Operations plan. The operations plan outlines how the business will be conducted and how the product or service will be produced. This section must include the general approach to operations, business location, facilities, and equipment.
10. Management team and company structure. This is a critical section of a business plan. Many investors and others who read business plans look first at the executive summary and then go directly to the management team section to assess the strength, experience and knowledge of the people spearheading the firm. It includes members of the management team, board of directors, board of advisors, and company structure. Whereas a board of directors is a panel of individuals elected by a corporation's shareholders to oversee the management of the firm, a board of advisors is a panel of experts used by a firm's board and management to provide counsel and advice on an ongoing basis. An organizational chart should be included in this section of the business plan which provides a graphical representa-

tion of how authority and responsibility are distributed within the company.

11. Risk analysis. Risk is a natural part of the entrepreneurial activity. A risk analysis seeks to identify the risks involved in starting the business and should outline the strategies to be implemented to counteract them. Major areas of risk include industry risk, technology and operational risk, financial risk, reputational risk, and personnel risk.
12. Overall schedule. A schedule should be prepared that shows the major events required to launch the business. The schedule should be in the format of milestones critical to the business's success.
13. Financial projections. This is the final section of a business plan and includes the firm's pro forma (or projected) financial statements which includes the income statement, balance sheet and cash flow statement. Having completed the previous sections of the plan, it's easy to understand why the financial projections come last. This section should detail the source of funding for the start-up capital required. The financial statements should be accompanied by detailed notes and assumptions to substantiate these projections. The strategies, goals, and objectives identified form the basis for the assumptions used to extrapolate pro forma income statements, pro forma balance sheets, pro forma cash flows, and sources and uses of funds statement.

A firm's pro forma financial statements are similar to the historical statements an established firm would normally prepare, except they are projections based on the goals and stategies contained in the plan. A cash flow or source and uses of funds statement is a document that lays out specifically how much money a firm would need, where the money will come from, and what the money will be used for. Ratio analysis is an important exercise that must be conducted to evaluate whether the projections are in line with industry standards and would identify if there are any outliers and the need to make changes in any assumptions used in preparation of the projections.

14. Appendix. Any material that does not easily fit into the body of a business plan but adds important information about the business should appear as an appendix.

The Oral Presentation of a Business Plan

In many instances it may be necessary to present the business plan to investors. When asked to meet with an investor, the founders of a new venture should prepare a set of PowerPoint slides that will fill the time slot allowed for the presentation. The first rule in making an oral presentation is to follow instructions. If an investor agrees with an entrepreneur that he or she has half an hour to make the presentation, stay within the time allocated, and leave some time for the investor to ask questions. The presentation should be smooth and well rehearsed. The slides should be sharp and not cluttered with material. Know yout business plan and hence the inherent risk if the business plan is prepared by a third party.

Questions and Feedback to Expect from Investors

1. Whether in the initial meeting or on subsequent occasions, an entrepreneur will be asked a host of questions by potential investors. The smart entrepreneur has a good idea of what to expect and is prepared for these questions or concerns. In this regard list a few potential questions and try to answer them so you would be fully prepared to answer any question on your business plan.
2. In the first meeting, investors typically focus on whether a real opportunity exists and whether the management team has the experience and skills to pull off the venture.

Updating the Business Plan

The business plan is usually updated for the following reasons:

- At the start of a new financial period
- When additional financing is needed
- When there has been a significant change in the market
- When a company launches a new product or service

- After a change in the management
- When the old plan no longer reflects the current state of the business

Guidelines to Prepare a Business Plan-An Outline Model

Executive summary:

An Executive Summary is a component of the business plan and details the following:

- Business concept (describe the business, its products, and the market, as well as identify the source of its competitive advantage)
- Financial features (sales, projected profit—income statement, balance sheet, and cash flow statement)
- Financial requirements clearly detail the start-up capital requirements by preparing a detailed listing of proposed capital expenditure and the source of equity funding

Business description:

- Short description of the company and industry and its present and future outlook
- Describe products the company intends to market and measures for success

Marketing and sales strategies:

- Define the market, marketing strategies (four Ps of marketing: Price, Product, Promotion, and Place and sales potential
- Planned distribution strategies
- Strategy for pricing, credit, and discount
- After-sales support, warranties, and product liability status

Competitor analysis:

- List the major competitors.
- Prepare a SWOT analysis (strengths, weaknesses, opportunities, and threats) of the business.
- List the strategies to be used to defend the company against competitors.
- List the opportunities and threats facing the business.
- List the major customers.
- Detail the rationale for the product or service.

Operations and management plan:

- List the key personnel, qualifications, experience, and training.
- Describe the major or key operations of the business.
- Prepare a detailed listing of all variable and fixed costs separately.
- List any specific methods of production/operations.
- List key or special skills required and if any special approval is required.
- List the raw materials required and whether local or imported. (This is particularly important owing to limited access to foreign exchange in Trinidad and Tobago and many Caribbean countries.)

Financial component:

- Projected monthly profit and loss statement, cash flow statement (first year) and balance sheet and projected annual statements for three years.

Collateral:

- List of items to be used/available as collateral, for example, equipment, machinery, household items, and so on
- Financial instruments, for example, fixed deposits, UTC shares, life insurance policies, and so on
- Real estate
- Vehicles
- Contract proceeds

One of the leading providers of finance and training for entrepreneurs in Trinidad and Tobago is the National Entrepreneurship Development Company Limited (NEDCO), which was established by the Government of Trinidad and Tobago in August 2002, as the implementing agency for government's policy on small and micro enterprise development. Links below provide detailed information on developing a business plan, and the "Key elements of a business plan—NEDCO" is available at:

http://www.nedco.gov.tt/Portals/y%200/Keelements%20of%20a%20Business%20Plan.pdf
http://www.entrepreneur.com/article/38308
http://www.forbes.com/sites/patrickhull/2013/02/21/10-essential-business-plan-components
http://smallbusiness.chron.com/key-elements-business-plan-56006.html

Discussion Cases

Case 1

Kristine Jacobs is a high school math teacher, who has created an iPhone app centered on engaging games that require high school students to use math to master the games. The idea is that the games are both appealing and will help students improve their math skills. Kristine has set aside the next two weekends to write a business plan. Do you think she's proceeding in the right manner?

Case 2

Jack and Jill Simpson just left their jobs with Microsoft to start a business that will sell a new type of entertainment equipment. They wrote a full business plan that they have asked you to review. When reading the plan, you noticed that several key sections start with the phrase "We believe…." Is any knowledgeable person who reads this plan going to know what "We believe…" really means? What is the problem with the statement "We believe…" in a business plan?

Case 3

Imagine you just received an e-mail message from a friend. The message reads, "Just wanted to tell you that I just finished writing my business plan. I'm very proud of it. It's very comprehensive and is just over 99 pages. The executive summary alone is 15 pages. I plan to start sending it out to potential investors next week." Do you have any words of advice for your friend? How would you respond to your friend's request for feedback?

Group Work

Suppose you have been asked by your local chamber of commerce to teach a two-hour workshop on how to write an effective business plan. The workshop will be attended by people who are thinking about starting their own business but do not currently have a business plan. Write a one-page outline detailing what you'd cover in the two-hour session.

The Elevator Pitch

When in business, you need to be prepared to talk about the business or business plan at any moment. A basic question, "So what do you do?" gives the entrepreneur the opportunity to sell the business. Marketers and investors call the response to this question your "elevator speech" because if prepared and crafted correctly, you can deliver it in the time it takes to ride an elevator through a high-rise building!

An elevator pitch should include:

- The business decription and solutions the business offers;
- Who would benefit;
- How big the market is; and
- Your qualifications to successfully manage and lead the organization.

Easy-to-Follow Elevator Pitch Template

Follow the elevator pitch template below and create a compelling elevator pitch for your business. Start with a clear mind and a blank sheet of paper. Each of the steps below asks you to write a very specific sentence or two, or in some cases, simply fill in the blanks of the sentence provided. For fill-in-the-blank sentences, the portions you are to supply are bracketed [like this].

1. [Name of your company] provides [your products or services] for [describe the specific segment of the market you will serve] who [describe the problem this solves for them].
2. [Enter one sentence that tells why this business is needed, what it offers and list the major customers.]
3. [Make a statement about the size and/or growth trend of the industry.]
4. [Write a sentence or two, no more, to address qualifications of the board and management to run the business.]
5. [Make an honest, upbeat, substantive, and credible claim about the business potential in terms of sales or profitability based on your industry analysis.]

How to Measure the Results of the Business Plan:
A business plan is based on historical data, analysis, and forecasts for the future. Mistakes can occur but preparing various simulations and measuring the implementation of the business plan can prevent catastrophic effects on the business. After commencement of the business it is important to compare the performance with the business plan. This includes:

- Objectives. This is important because if the objectives are not achieved, it needs review to determine if changes are necessary in order to achieve the goals.
- Products/services. Has the company introduced products or services listed in the business plan? What are the results when compared with the products or services of the competitors? Does the company have

plans to introduce new products or services that were not included in the business plan?

- Market. What is the feedback from the market? What is the level of customer service? What action is required to improve its brand and image?
- Industry. Are there any major changes in the industry that were not predicted in your business plan? What are the plans to service the industry in a more meaningful way?
- Marketing strategy. Are there changes in the marketing strategy that are not covered in the business plan? How effective is the price, promotion, and distribution policy? List changes that must be included in the revised plan.
- Sales. Is the sales in line with the business plan or variance less than 10%? What needs to be done to improve sales?
- Marketing plan. If a relook of the business requires some marketing changes, update the business plan.
- Structure. Does the organizational structure need revising? The plan should be modified to reflect a revised structure if necessary.
- Profit/Loss. Is the profit/loss statement within 10% of the current business plan? A review of the goals, objectives and strategies would be necessary if there is a substantial shortfall in profit.
- Cash flow. Is your cash flow in line with projections? If there is any shortfall, measures needs to be put in place to finance the shortfall.
- SWOT analysis. Are there changes in the strengths, weakness, opportunities, and threats as detailed in the business plan? The plan needs to be amended to reflect the new goals and strategies that must be implemented.

In summary the process of measurement of the business plan includes the comparison of actual performance with budget (as per business plan), investigation of variances, and early introduction of revised strategies to reduce or eliminate negative differences.

Index

A
Accounting, 177, 193, 200
The Accounting cycle, 211–214
Account number, 46
Accounts, 36, 40–46, 55, 56
Accrued revenues, expenses, 222
Activity ratios, 226–228
Agreement, 135, 136, 138, 139, 148, 158, 159, 166, 171–173
Amount of settlement, 169
Annual depreciation expense, 219, 220
Annual General Meeting, 45
Annual Return, 45
Annuities, 38, 39, 69, 75
Asset, 209, 212, 213, 215, 216, 218–223, 225, 226, 228
Attorney, 134, 138, 139, 142–144, 147, 148, 155, 172
Australia, 1, 14, 17
Avoidance, 23–26

B
Bank account, 46
Bankers and creditors, 208
Bankers' Association of Trinidad and Tobago (BATT), 152, 155
Barbados, 1, 14
Baseline survey, 8–9, 18
Bonds, 38, 41
Brainstorming, 185, 186
Budget, 22, 26, 30–32
Budgeting, 30–32, 75
Business plan, 231–248

C
Campus Chapter Habitat for Humanity, 5
Capital, 40, 210–212, 214, 217, 226
Caribbean, 133

C. Sahadeo, *Financial Literacy and Money Script*,
https://doi.org/10.1007/978-3-319-77075-8

Caribbean Institute of Media and Communication (CARIMAC), 12–13
Central Bank, 3
Central Bank and Financial Institutions (Non-Banking Amendment) Act 1986, 83, 84
Central Bank of Trinidad and Tobago (CBTT), 3–4, 6–10
Central Depository, 41
Certificate of Insurance, 99–103, 117
Characteristics, 176
Colonial Life Insurance Company Limited (CLICO), 6–8
Commercial banks, 36
Competitor, 239, 240, 244, 247
Comprehensive, 92–95, 97–99, 105, 111, 117, 118, 121, 124, 128
Comprehensive motor insurance, 93–94
Construction loan, 161–165
Contract, 131, 134–136, 138, 148–155, 159, 160, 164–167, 171, 172
Copyright, 187, 188
Corporate and government bonds, 69, 74
Covenants, 132, 151
Creative process, 185–186
Creativity, 176, 181–185
Credit card, 57–64
Credit rating, 63, 64
Credits, 210, 211, 212, 213, 215–218, 266, 227
Cross-border transfers, 44
Current Accounts, 36
Customer service support, 191–192, 200

D

Debit card, 64, 65
Debits, 211, 212, 213, 215–218
Debt service ratio (DSR), 137, 146, 150, 157–158
Debt-to-income, 58
Deed, 132, 133, 136, 138–140, 142–145, 147–151, 154–156, 158, 159, 163, 164
Deed of conveyance, 136, 139, 140, 142, 147, 159
Deposit Insurance, 81–91
Deposit Insurance Company (DIC), 82–87, 89–91
Depositors, 82–91
Deposits, 44, 81, 126
Deposit transfer, 90
Depreciation, 211, 219, 220, 221, 223, 227
Direct deposit, 46
Distribution, 192, 200
Dividend yield, 55

E

Earnings per share (EPS), 52, 54, 55
Education, vii
Emotional Intelligence (EI), 203–205
Empathy, 204, 205
Employer, 70–72, 78
Employer's pension, 70–72
Entrepreneur, viii, 175–182, 184, 185, 187–189, 193, 203
Entrepreneurial firms, 177, 179–181
Entrepreneurial process, 180–181, 189
Entrepreneurial pursuits, 40, 69, 75
Entrepreneurship, viii

Equity-based, 40
Equity-based mutual funds, 69, 72, 74
Expenses, 35, 209, 212–215, 217–220, 222, 223, 229
External auditors, 208

F

Fees, 60
Finance charge, 60
Financial crisis, 2
Financial goals, 68, 69
Financial independence, 1–2
Financial institutions, 4, 36, 43, 44, 49
Financial literacy, ix
Financial planning, 69
Fixed assets, 209, 210, 212, 219, 220, 227, 228
Fixed deposit, 36, 38, 40, 69
Fixed rate mortgage, 149, 150
Focus group, 186–187
Foreign Exchange Deposits, 36
Fraud, 63, 64
Full third party, 95
Function administration, 191

G

Goals, 21–32, 231–233, 235, 241, 247, 248
Good credit rating, 63–64
Good root of title, 134–140
Government, 208
Grace period, 60, 61
Guarantors, 135, 146–147, 148

H

Habitat for Humanity, 5
Healthy, 23, 24, 27
Hire purchase, 59–60, 63
Home, 82, 103, 116
Home equity, 167
Homeownership, *see* Entrepreneur
Human resource (HR), 191, 193–194, 200

I

Incentives and rewards, 60, 61
Income, 35, 36, 38, 39, 48, 54, 68–70, 72–76, 209, 211, 213, 219, 220, 222–224, 229
Independence, 131
Industry, 238, 241, 243, 247, 248
Industry analysis, 238, 247
Information and Communication Technology (ICT), 194–195, 200
Initial Public Offering (IPO), 49–53
Innovation, 179–182
Installment, 59–60
Instruments, 38–40
Insurance, 81, 91, 92, 94–106, 108–117
Insurance coverage, 83, 85–88, 100, 117
Insured deposits, 89–90
Interventions, 7, 9, 10, 16
Investment, 36–41, 48, 50–53, 81, 83, 91, 92
Investment bank, 50, 51
Investor, 41

J

Jamaica, 1, 10–12
Joint accounts, 84, 87–89
Joint ownership, 47

K

Key benchmarks, 52–53

L

Launch, 3, 4
Ledger, 212, 213, 215, 216, 217
Letters of administration/grant of probate, 46
Legal department, 194
Liability, 209, 212, 213, 215, 221, 225
Liability to third party, 95
Life, 81, 82, 91, 111
Life cycle, 29
Life insurance, 81, 82, 91–92
Liquidator, 85, 86, 90
Liquidity ratios, 224–226
Loan accounts, 90
Loans, 57–59, 63
Loan to Value ratio (LTV), 137, 135, 138

M

Main account, 56
Management, 57–65
Market, 231, 233, 234, 237–240, 242, 243, 246–248
Market analysis, 238–239
Marketing plan, 240, 248
Mind mapping, 186
Mission, 232–235, 238
Money avoidance, 23–26
Money market funds, 38, 40, 69, 74
Money script, 21–32
Money status, 23–25
Money vigilance, 23, 27
Money worship, 23–25
Mortgage, 133–139, 141–161, 164–169, 172
Mortgage contract, 148–154, 165–167
Mortgage Installment Protection Plan, 167
Mortgage loan, 136, 137, 138, 139, 146, 148, 149, 150, 166, 168
Mortgage Market Reference Rate (MMRR), 153–155
Motivation, 176, 204
Motor vehicle, 92, 119
Motor vehicle insurance, 92–116
Mutual funds, 38, 40
Myths, 73

N

National Financial Education Programme (NFEP), 14
National Financial Literacy, 3–4, 16
National Financial Literacy programme (NFLP), 3–4, 8, 9
National Insurance, 38
National Insurance Board (NIB), 75
Net profit, 209, 210, 211, 213, 214
New Zealand, 1, 14–16, 19
No Claim Discount (NCD), 98–100, 102, 114

O

Old age pension, 75, 76
Operations plan, 240
Ordinary Savings Account, 36
Owner's equity, 209–211, 215

P

Passion, 176
Patent, 187, 188
Pension, 38, 68, 70–73, 75, 76, 78
Plan, 231–233, 235–247
Pledges, 41, 43, 44
Policy excess or deductible, 97
Power of attorney, 46
Price earnings ratio (P/E), 54–55
Production, 191, 197–199, 200
Profit, 208–211, 213, 214, 217, 219, 227–229
Profitability ratios, 228–229
Property insurance, 116–129
Property value coverage, 168–170
Protecting intellectual property, 188
Public intervention, 10

R

Real Property Act (RPA), 143, 144, 155
Registrar of Companies, 45
Registrar services, 44
Regulators, 208, 209
Rental agreement, 171–173
Research and development (R & D), 180, 199–202
Retirement, 3, 67–79
Retirement benefits, 68, 74–77
Retirement fund, 68, 69, 71, 72, 74–75
Revenue, 209–211, 213, 214, 215, 217, 218, 219, 221, 222, 223
Risks, 40

S

Sales, 178, 187, 191, 193, 195, 196–198, 200
Savings, 35, 68–70, 73, 74
Savings account, 56
Securities, 40, 131–133, 136, 138, 143, 148–150, 158, 164, 170, 172, 173
Securities and Exchange Commission (SEC), 41, 49–51
Self-awareness (SA), 203, 204, 205
Self-regulation, 204, 205
Senior Citizen grant, 72, 76
Service mark, 188
Shareholders, 39, 41, 44–47, 49, 51, 54, 208, 225, 226, 228
Shares, 36, 39–51, 53–55, 69, 72, 74
S.M.A.R.T., 28
S.M.A.R.T goals, 28
Social skill (SS), 204, 205
Sources, 68, 69, 72–75
Stamp duty, 142–145
Statement, 43, 50, 51, 56
Stockbroker, 41–44, 48, 49, 53
Stock exchange, 42, 48–51
Stocks, 38–44, 46, 47, 49–51, 53–55, 69, 72, 74
Strategies, 231, 233–235, 237–241, 243, 244, 248
Sum insured, 95, 97, 101, 105, 115, 118, 119, 121–123, 125, 126, 129
Survey, 8, 9, 16–18
SWOT, 232, 233, 238, 244, 248

T

Time Savings Deposit Account, 36
Third party insurance, 92, 94
Total Debt Service Ratio, 157
Transfers, 44
Trademark, 187, 188
Treasury bills, 38, 40, 69, 74
Trial balance, 213, 214, 216–223
Trinidad and Tobago, 1–4, 6–8, 19
Trinidad and Tobago Central Depository (TTCD), 41–48
Trinidad and Tobago Stock Exchange (TTSE), 41, 47, 49, 51
Turnover, 226, 227, 228

U

Unhealthy, 23–27
United Kingdom (UK), 1, 14, 18, 19
University of the West Indies (UWI), 4–8, 12

V

Value Added Tax (VAT), 104, 106
Vision, 232, 233, 235, 238

W

Withdrawals, 40, 44
Words, 31

CPSIA information can be obtained
at www.ICGtesting.com
Printed in the USA
LVOW13*2100220618
581599LV00013B/343/P